TRAVELING BLIND

The Journey Toward Future Joy and a Deeper Christian Faith as a Survivor of Suicide

by

Letty Lozano

Geron GA & Associates

Watercress Press
111 Grotto Blvd.
San Antonio, Texas, 78216
www.watercresspress.com

Dedication

I dedicate this book to all people everywhere who have lost a loved one. I hope that by sharing my story, others will gain a sense of peace, hope, and acceptance. Life does go on for those of us that are left behind, but we must first go through it in order to get through it.

I pay tribute to Bert for the wonderful memories left behind that have made us who we are and who we continue to become. I believe that although he is no longer here physically, he will always live on in spirit through all the people whose lives he touched.

I want to thank my family and friends for the love, support, and encouragement that was always abundantly available. I will never forget their thoughts, prayers, and acts of kindness when I needed them the most.

I also want to thank my editor, Nancy Johanson, who went above and beyond her work as my editor. Not only did she help write the words that were in my heart, her belief in me and my story inspired me to continue when I wanted to give up. I would also like to thank my niece, Regan Perez, for the use of her photographs.

Most of all, I want to thank God for never leaving my side. By His grace and mercy He filled me with the courage and strength I never knew I had. It was in the darkest days that I was traveling blind. He took my hand and led me out of the darkness and into the light with Him. I continue with my life, not sure where I am going, but I have faith and trust in God that He knows what He is doing. I continue to witness miracles and accept with gratitude the blessings He continues to put in my path, Thank you God, for everything!

Letty Lozano
San Antonio, 2012

Table of Contents

Prologue   1

Chapter 1: Shock and Mind-numbing Sorrow   5

Chapter 2: Saying Adieu   15

Chapter 3: Signs of Hope   25

Chapter 4: Breaking the Barrier of Silence   32

Chapter 5: One Step Forward, Two Steps Back   50

Chapter 6: Memories and Mayhem   65

Chapter 7: Lingering Doubts   76

Chapter 8: Truth and Trust   85

Chapter 9: Coping with Celebrations   97

Chapter 10: Dreams, Decisions, and Death   107

Chapter 11: Remembering, Persevering, Renewing   123

Chapter 12: Curative Comfort   135

Epilogue   144

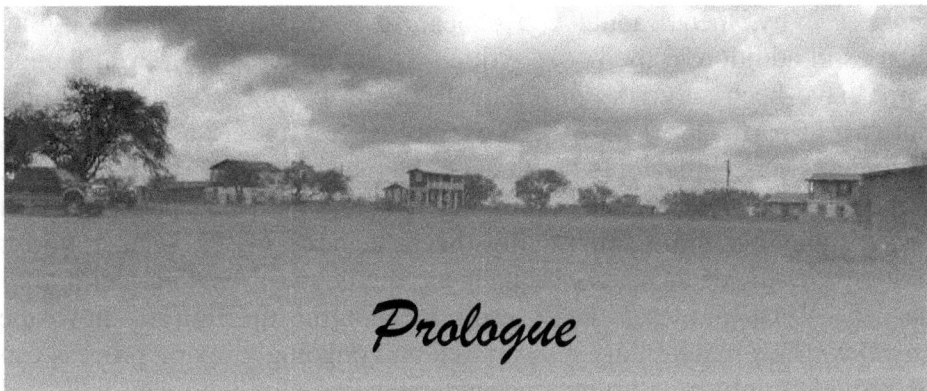

Prologue

W e've heard the words and phrases spoken by many adults since our early childhoods. Death is no respecter of persons. The old, the young, the rich, the poor, the educated or uneducated . . . everyone eventually faces death. Live today as though it were your last. Be grateful for every sunrise; it means you're still alive. We've attended the funerals of relatives, friends, and acquaintances. Some died of old age, some of longtime serious illness, some from a tragic accident, some as a soldier serving our country. We've read a plethora of newspaper accounts and watched daily reports on television of the senseless murders of countless people. We know that death can come quickly, unexpectedly, after a long period of suffering, or when the heart simply gives out due to old age. We accept all of this. Death is part of the reality of life.

But never, as a parent or spouse or child or sibling, do we expect the end of life for someone we love to come through suicide. Death by suicide was never part of *our* reality.

Until now.

I am a survivor of a suicide, just like you. My husband chose to end his life.

Right away, you should know I'm not a psychiatrist, a psychologist, a psychotherapist, a mental health counselor specializing in crisis intervention, or a facilitator of group therapy for those who need the support of others experiencing persistent trauma during their mourning

1

process. Why, then, should you choose to read *Traveling Blind*, rather than or in addition to the books written by the professionals, even though some have been survivors of a suicide themselves? For several reasons, but two in particular: I have been exactly where you are now, struggling to find answers while coping with even the most menial of daily activities, wanting to blame someone, but living with the guilt that perhaps I was responsible; but more importantly, because none of the secular books written for suicide survivors brought me the depth of healing and hope I needed. What did they lack? Any meaningful mention of how the *comforting* we require during our initial and ongoing grieving process can be provided only by a loving and understanding God who can, will, and does supply it. Continually and in abundance.

God says, "I am here." He's waiting for us to come to Him. His arms are opened wide, and once they enfold us, we know this is a Comforter who will never leave, who will never be too busy, who understands our pain without our ever having to spell it out, and who will provide all the answers we need and want . . . in time, when we're ready. He knows we can't stand tall and move steadily forward with courage until we've first been comforted.

> So do not fear, for I am with you; do not be dismayed, for I am your God. I will strengthen you and help you; I will uphold you with my righteous right hand. — Isaiah 41:10 (NIV)

Suicide produces a lonely grief. One that is only temporarily eased by all the hugs and compassionate platitudes from dear friends and other family members, neighbors and work colleagues who come for the first few days or weeks after our personal tragedy is made known. They offer their support through a variety of caring and welcome assistance. However, in our alone moments and during the long sleepless nights when our questions and guilt and depression plague us, and long after their helpful presence has diminished as they get on with their own lives, we agonize over our loss in a soul-wrenching grief that leaves us feeling hollow and apathetic. The hole in our soul can't be repaired by hearing or

2

reading the statistics regarding how often suicides occur in our country, by sharing our feelings with those who lend an ear — including the professionals we may need to provide a temporary fix of antidepressant medications — or by reading several fact-filled books that focus on the phases of grief and how they will eventually fade in intensity.

We hear. We read. We endlessly share. But nothing seems to work. We are left reaching into the dark for that "something" or "someone" who can lessen the pain and provide the impetus to move forward with renewed energy and even enthusiasm.

Of course, that someone is God. But our shock and ensuing anger produced a lessoning of our faith as our finger of blame pointed directly at Him. We decided *He* allowed the suicide to happen and it wasn't fair. We even think He made it happen to punish us for a wrongdoing. We "travel blind," like Job of the Old Testament, when we don't understand that God is hurting just as much as we are, or that violence and wars and debilitating diseases and, yes, suicide are the results of Satan's testing of our faith. We have been granted free will by God to make our own decisions, and when we consciously or unconsciously leave Him out of our lives, we usually make the wrong ones.

When all else failed, I finally turned back to God, who was waiting patiently for me and understood my anger and frustration and forgave me. In Him I found the comfort I needed.

> *Come to me, all you who are weary and burdened, and I will give you rest. Take my yoke upon you and learn from me, for I am gentle and humble in heart, and you will find rest for your souls. For my yoke is easy and my burden is light.* — Matthew 11:28-30 (NIV)

It is my hope that when you choose to read *Traveling Blind*, you will also find the comfort that only God can provide and, in time, the answers to all your questions. The journey takes time and involves many twists and turns. But every step of the way back to your peace of mind will be filled with God's reassuring presence.

I am reminded of the words of encouragement written by the well-known author Annie Johnson Flint back in 1919. Although her body was twisted through the crippling effects of arthritis most of her life, her incessant pain and suffering made her more sensitive to the anguish of others. I offer her words to you now, because they echo those of the Apostle Paul, who reminded us that God has never promised us a trouble-free life, only that His "grace is sufficient" and His "strength is made perfect" in our weakness. (II Cor. 12:9, NIV)

What God Hath Promised

God hath not promised skies always blue,
Flower strewn pathways all our lives through;
God hath not promised sun without rain,
Joy without sorrow, peace without pain.

God hath not promised we shall not know
Toil and temptation, trouble and woe;
He hath not told us we shall not bear
Many a burden, many a care.

God hath not promised smooth roads and wide,
Swift, easy travel, needing no guide;
Never a mountain rocky and steep,
Never a river turbid and deep.

But God *hath* promised strength for the day,
Rest for the labor, light for the way,
Grace for the trials, help from above,
Unfailing sympathy, undying love.

It is my prayer that as you read my story, you will find similarities to your own and decide to take your own journey back to faith in order to find renewed happiness in the months and years to come. Life *does* go on for the living, and God wants us to savor every minute of it.

Letty Lozano

Chapter 1

Shock and Mind-numbing Sorrow

When daily rituals are unexpectedly interrupted, our door of contentment flies open to let in the unwelcome voices of apprehension and concern. Not even the restful beauty of the vista I usually enjoyed from the backyard deck of our San Antonio home brought me the peace of mind I needed on the Wednesday morning of May 6, 2009. I stared sightlessly into space, thinking and worrying. An hour or so earlier, I had placed a call to Joel, one of my husband's co-workers, asking him to drive out to a ranch near Laredo where my husband Bert had said he would make a short visit before going to work in town. I hadn't spoken with Bert since Tuesday morning. Twenty-four hours of silence.

Those inner voices returned and spoke louder to me this time, raising all sorts of anxious thoughts. Bert had never missed a day without calling me.

For eight years, Bert had worked in Laredo as the chief engineer for a cold storage company during the week while living in a house he had built for us on my parents' ranch, about forty-five miles outside Laredo. He had also leased some land from a friend of his about ten miles from Laredo, where he kept cattle. He'd spend almost every weekend with our two children and me in San Antonio, or I'd spend the weekend down there. This particular week, he had taken Monday off, which was unusual for him, as he rarely missed work. When I spoke with his co-worker, he'd said, "You know, he never showed up for work yesterday either, Letty."

Two days? Bert had been insistent that he needed to return to Laredo on Tuesday in our conversation early that morning. My thoughts raced through several possibilities. Had he been in a car accident? But why hadn't the police notified me? Maybe he'd forgotten to recharge his cellphone. Maybe he'd had a heart attack or a stroke and couldn't use his phone and was —

The cellphone beside me interrupted my thoughts. As I snatched it up and brought the receiver to my ear, my heart accelerated, pounding so hard I could hear and feel it.

"Letty? I found him," Joel said, his voice conflicted with unspilled emotion. "I'm so sorry. He's . . . he's dead!"

"What?" I whispered. *"Dead?"* I choked on the word. "But . . . how?"

"He took his life, Letty. Shot himself in the head."

My heart stopped and the phone slipped from my hand. As if in slow motion, I fell to my knees, feeling the blood drain from my head, making me dizzy and unable to think. *"No, no, no. Please, no! Tell me it's not true. It's not true."* I knew the wailing words were coming from my mouth, but all I could hear in my head was, "He's dead. He took his life. He's dead. He took his life. *He took his life.*"

From that moment and for the next several hours, I was in another world; a world where humans who become instant zombies go when they're unable to deal with the new reality that has just been handed them. I was told later that when we suffer from a traumatic situation as devastating as the declaration of a suicide by a loved one, our minds go instantly into denial, an unconscious coping mechanism that gives us time to adjust and to absorb the shocking information.

Thankfully, Sonya was in my home watching over my elderly parents who had lived with us for two years. She heard my screams and rushed outdoors to pick up the phone from the deck and obtain the rest of the information from Joel.

Forgotten by me at the time, I had received a call from my friend Ana that morning, right after I had called Joel. I had relayed my concern about Bert's not calling me or answering my calls to him. Sharing my same apprehension, she had decided to come for a visit of support. She arrived immediately after the fateful call and cradled me in her arms as I sobbed uncontrollably. "Oh, Ana, what am I going to do? How can I possibly live without my Bert?" I could hear the gut-wrenching cries and knew they were coming from me, but I couldn't stop them. It was like I had turned on the faucet of pain and the force of the emotional gush left me too weak to turn it off.

I didn't know that when he left for work Tuesday morning, it would be the last time I'd ever see my husband alive. Had Bert known? Is that why he'd stayed home on Monday, rather than returning to Laredo? To spend one more day with the kids and me? Had he premeditated his suicide? For how long? And why? When I think of it now, I'm surprised such questions found their way into my consciousness, I was such an emotional wreck. I thought I was having a heart attack. I couldn't think. Couldn't breathe. I was in a full-blown state of panic.

Very early Tuesday morning, I was still lying in bed while watching Bert buckle his belt and lift his arms so that his heavily starched shirt would give him some wiggle room. "I wish you didn't have to leave, honey. Can't you stay home just one more day?" I'd asked wistfully, knowing the answer before it was given.

"I have to go now," he'd said, rather bluntly.

Bert and I were accustomed to the goodbyes every week, although we didn't like them. Usually, while hugging me, he'd say, "You know how much I hate to leave you, but I have to make a living. I love you and before we know it, it'll be Friday and I'll be back here with you."

In my eyes, Bert was the most handsome man in the world. From his Justin lace-up work boots to the top of his black felt cowboy hat, in his wranglers and long-sleeved button-down shirt, and always, no matter what, a white tee shirt under it, he was a picture of rugged manhood. But it was his eyes, his ready smile and infectious laugh that appealed to me most.

Ana had steered me back into the house. Through the fog of my emotional stress, I knew I had something important to do. I dreaded it and wished I could wave it away or have Ana take over for me, but it was my responsibility. My twenty-year old son, Christopher, was still asleep. A student at a local university, he was in finals week and had the day off. I needed to tell him, before he heard it from someone else. I made my way to his bedroom, dreading my task, and finally stood over him, choking on my tears. "Christopher, wake up, honey!" I sank onto the edge of his bed and became overwhelmed with having to be the messenger of such unfathomable news about his stepfather, who'd loved him since he was six years old.

I peered at my son as he opened his eyes and then blurted out the news before I could think rationally about the effect it would have on him. "Bert's dead, Christopher! They said he . . . he took his life down on the ranch. Oh, son . . . what are we going to do without him?" Holding my hands to my heart as if to keep it from breaking through the walls of my chest, I released explosions of sobs that scared even me and had Christopher leaping from his bed in a state of total disbelief and shock of his own.

"What are you saying, Mom? It's not true! Bert would never do that. If he's dead, then somebody killed him!"

I watched him pace back and forth in front of me, not knowing what to do or where to go, as his own cries joined mine. At that moment, I couldn't help him. My own pain and state of mind prevented me from thinking of anyone else's agony. Even my son's. We held each other and finally decided we needed to know the details. Only then could we begin to accept the cold hard truth. We joined Sonya on the back deck where she had been talking to Joel on the phone.

"This is what Joel told me, Letty. After arriving at the ranch, he drove up to the cattle pens where he saw your husband's green Ford truck. He said he parked and felt a sense of relief. You know, that your husband was there. He saw him lying on the other side of the truck and thought he had truck problems. He walked over to him to help out and that's when . . . that's when he saw what had happened. He . . . he was panic-stricken. Your husband . . . he was face down, like he had been kneeling on the dirt before . . . putting the g-gun to his head."

The next hours were a total blur. I shut out any vision of Bert on the ground by his truck. Sonya had already called members of my immediate

8

family and in a state of total numbness, after Ana's encouragement, I gathered enough courage to call Bert's sister and his mother. Then I remembered that earlier that morning I had also called Bert's best friend Noe, who had headed down to Laredo as soon as I told him I hadn't heard from Bert since Tuesday morning. Now, I called him to relay the news.

"That doesn't sound like Bert," he said. "He can't possibly be dead. I'm almost there. Don't worry, Letty. It's not true. I'll call you when I get there."

"Thank you so much," I said. "I . . . I'll wait to hear from you." I felt hopeful. Maybe it wasn't Bert after all. Maybe it was someone else. Joel had made a mistake and jumped to conclusions, because of the horror he'd seen. Maybe it was the friend Bert had mentioned to me; the one who was going to help find a calf that had been missing for the auction. Maybe an intruder had arrived, killed the friend, and kidnapped Bert for ransom.

In only a few short minutes, my phone rang. "Letty," Noe said, "I apologize for raising your hopes. It's Bert all right. I'm so sorry."

Word spread quickly. Within the hour, people began arriving at the house and echoed my cries of agony, hugging each other while uttering the same word I continued to repeat. "Why? *Why?"* Walking about aimlessly, I didn't know what to do with myself. *"Where do I go? What should I do? What happens next?"* It was as if I were outside my body looking down at a stranger. I wanted to die, the pain was so intense. Over and over again, the same words poured from my mouth as though my voice box were a CD stuck in the same groove. "I don't want to live. I want to be with Bert."

Christopher listened to me and finally had enough. With a look that pierced my heart, he shouted, "Shut up, Mom! Stop saying that!"

Someone told me that Noe would spend the night in Laredo and return the next day with Bert's body, once it had been released from the county morgue. *"Body?"* What were they talking about? How dare they talk about Bert as though he were nothing more than a . . . a carcass!

Then I heard snippets of other conversation. "His spirit will always be with us."

It was a kind thing to say under the circumstances, but the words didn't bring any sense of comfort. I wanted Bert's body and his spirit to remain intact, so that when he returned to San Antonio I could feel his arms around me and hear his declaration of love.

I vaguely remember hearing my sisters talk quietly with each other. "She needs some sort of medication to calm her down. Her hysteria will make her ill."

My ears perked up. Maybe I could swallow an entire bottle of pills and die that way. Only death could alleviate my anguish. Now, I'm so thankful there were people around me at all times. I was in no state of mind to process the situation or control my frenzied reaction to it.

I wanted everyone to leave the house so I could think; but, at the same time, I was afraid they would and my sense of abandonment would grow worse. My mind raced through a series of disjointed thoughts and I was unable to make sense of any of them. When had Bert called me last? Oh, yes. It was on Tuesday only a couple of hours after he had left the house for Laredo. What had we talked about? What had he said that should have caught my attention? I had been in my car when my cellphone rang. I knew it was Bert from the special ring.

"I was just calling you to see what you were doing," he'd said. Now, in retrospect, I should have heard the flatness in his voice. Not like the Bert I knew so well.

"Just running errands." I could remember exactly where I was when his call came to me, but not where I was going.

"Before I go in to work, I'm going to stop by the ranch."

I knew without his saying so that it wasn't our ranch with the house, but the one where he kept his cattle. A few weeks before, he had sold the whole herd, as we needed the money.

"I'm meeting a friend who's going to help me find a calf that was missing when I took the rest of the herd to auction." He paused. "I don't know if I'll have enough gas to make it back to town."

I remember wondering why he didn't just stop for gas first, but at least his friend would be there. I have analyzed that comment over and over again in my mind. What, exactly, had he meant? Was it his way of telling me where he could be found? Later. When his calls stopped coming. When he'd fulfilled his real mission.

If I had been more inquisitive and asked more questions and really listened to the answers, could I have figured out he wasn't himself and sent help before it was too late? Then came the thought that plagues me to this day. Why hadn't he told me he loved me, if he knew this was his last phone call to me. Every phone call we'd ever had ended with, "I love you." Not this time. Was I too busy watching traffic to notice? Too distracted by the purpose of my errand? Too accustomed to our weekly routine to make each moment of conversation meaningful?

After the investigation of Bert's death was completed, my brother-in-law, Roy, picked up Bert's truck at the police storage for impounded vehicles. The gas gauge showed a quarter of a tank remained. Was Bert trying to tell me that *he* was out of gas — that he was just plain tuckered out and couldn't dig himself out of the ditch of pain or fear he was in? There was no evidence to suggest anyone else had been at the ranch or that there was a missing calf. He had purposely lied to me, probably thinking he was saving me from a future filled with the same anxiety that had driven him over the edge.

The hours flew by in what seemed like a lifetime for me. I vaguely remembered that Emily, my fourteen-year old daughter, would be coming home from school. Bert had been a wonderful stepdad to her . . . to both of my children. Their father and I had gone through a difficult and painful divorce when Christopher was six and Emily not even a year old. Thinking of Emily and Christopher made me feel instantly angry. Not at Bert. At God. How could He let something like this happen? We'd been through enough as a family already. It wasn't fair. My heart swelled with bitterness and resentfulness. God had abandoned Bert and me. All of us. What happened to His promise not to give us more than we could bear? Well, this was way over the top. He should have known I couldn't bear to live without Bert.

Unknown to me at the time, Ana had driven to the school to pick up Emily, saying only that there was a family emergency. My sisters — Elsa, Laura, and Lisa — waited at the door for her arrival, wanting to soften the blow of my emotional condition. Christopher bolted halfway down the driveway to meet her. He struggled to get out the words through his tears. "Emily, there's been an accident. Bert was shot. He . . . he's *dead*!"

Immediately, Emily burst into tears. My sisters ran out to meet her and provided all the hugs and comforting I was unable to give her. By now, they had consulted with our family physician and administered an antidepressant to calm me down. I was in my own vaporous world, breathing, but not alive to the reality playing out in my own home. I watched and listened through a drugged stupor, but could offer nothing coherent or substantive.

If it weren't for the tears, one would have thought the Lozano family was having a big family reunion or house party. More people arrived with food and flowers and voices of concern. My sister Lisa was in continual touch with the Laredo investigators. My sister Elsa and sister-in-law Pearl were huddled together making the funeral arrangements. Their attempts to include me had been futile.

Larry — Christopher and Emily's father — came by to pay his respects and so did his father, Henry, my ex father-in-law. I was slumped on the couch, unable to respond with any sense of gratitude for their presence, when Henry came to sit beside me. "You need to be careful about what you say around the kids, Letty. Your saying you want to die, too, could have some lasting consequences on their well-being."

I heard the depth of his concern and nodded. "I understand what you're telling me, Henry, but I can't help how I feel. That's how I feel right now. I can't imagine my life without Bert."

Henry patted me. "I know what you're going through, but try to keep those feelings to yourself. For the kids." He had lost his wife suddenly, not long after Larry and I had married, and knew firsthand of the pain that comes with the loss of a loved one.

As the day progressed, I felt physically and emotionally exhausted. If I couldn't die I wished I could lapse into a deep sleep. I didn't want to think or feel anything anymore. As people left for their homes, I dreaded being alone. I asked my sister Laura if she would stay the night and sleep with Emily and me in what used to be Bert's and my bed. I couldn't bear the thought of sleeping there without my husband by my side.

Laura agreed and took Bert's side in our bed. Emily slept between us. She didn't want to be alone with her thoughts either. By then, all I wanted to do was protect her and help her feel safe. I wanted to muffle the chaos. We had cried until there were no more tears left . . . at least for that day. Maybe upon awakening, things would be different. Maybe the entire day was only a nightmare and we'd greet a new day with things the way they'd always been.

For a long time I remained sleepless, as a movie of Bert's last hours with me played over and over again in my mind. Then the intrusive scenario of his arrival at the ranch and what happened next deepened my anguish. I imagined his exiting the truck, pulling the gun from under the car seat or wherever he had stashed it, and slamming the truck door. I wondered what was going through his mind. Had he thought of me? Of his own son? Of my two children? Of how we'd take the news of his death? Of how we'd manage financially without his support? Had he been as numb to our pain as he was to his own? As I was now? Was he too deep into a clinical depression to think rationally? Had he divorced himself from reality, as I was doing?

Even though I was far from believing God even existed at this point, I prayed out of habit. "Please, God, don't let this be real. Erase this day from my memory and return things to normal. Let this be a nightmare that will vanish with the arrival of dawn."

My soul is weary with sorrow; strengthen me according to your word.
— Psalm 19:28 (NIV)

Chapter 2

Saying Adieu

After a fitful sleep, I dragged myself from the bed to be hit once again by the harsh truth. Nothing had changed. Bert would never come home . . . not ever again. I didn't want to think about it. If I admitted to his death, I'd have to fret over the whys and about who'd take care of all the tasks that had been his responsibility. I'd have to think about the consequences that would surely follow and have a profound effect on my life and that of our children. I'd have to think about his funeral and accompanying expenses and simply sitting through the service. I wasn't ready for any of that.

The thought came to me that I should forget about myself and focus on the welfare of my parents, who walked the house with haunted eyes; Bert's parents, who must be in the same state of denial and distress; his son, Bert Michael, who lived in Mexico with his mother and would have to learn of his father's suicide over the phone; and my two devastated children, but I was paralyzed against taking any meaningful action. I wondered, briefly, if anyone had contacted Bert's boss in Laredo, although somewhere in the back of my mind I knew Joel had informed him. I brushed away thinking about anything that would require my having to make a decision and then carrying it out. Even the smallest task seemed overwhelming in scope, like getting dressed or combing my hair. My mind flitted from one thought to the next, never tarrying long enough to make an impact.

My children were ghosts of their former selves, staring furtively at me to judge my state of mind, wondering if I would become hysterical again. I wanted to be strong for them, to be their comforter, but seemed utterly detached from my former self. The tears were still quick to come, hovering on my eyelids and spilling over to run down my cheeks at unexpected times. They seemed to have a will of their own. It felt like my heart had lodged in my throat, making any attempt to speak in a normal voice impossible. I wanted to remain medicated so I wouldn't have to participate in any of the activities of others, knowing I couldn't survive another day without the numbing effect of the tranquilizers. The only thing I wanted to do, until the requisite funeral services, was sleep. Sleeping was the only way I could escape the severity of my emotional pain.

My sisters and other family members spent those first couple of days taking care of every task that should have been mine. They selected a coffin and made plans for the burial. They met with St. Mark's parish priest regarding the funeral service and with those in charge of the Mission Park South mortuary chapel where the Rosary service would be held. They wrote an obituary and contacted the local newspaper.

When the day of the Rosary service arrived, I used every ounce of energy I had to dress in the black outfit a sister had helped me select from my closet and to apply a modicum of makeup. I would have attended in my pajamas if I'd had a choice. As I entered the funeral home through the side door, the first people I saw were Bert's parents. I had not seen them during the first two days of chaos and after my initial call to his mother. Our families are big and perhaps we felt comfort in grieving in our own familiar home settings. The pain in their eyes and on their faces mirrored my own. I hugged my father-in-law tightly, as if I were holding Bert. We both cried in that deep sorrowful blubbering that comes from the core of your being. "Bert will always be with us," he said, when he could finally speak.

"I . . . I just want him to come h-home," I wailed. As I stepped aside to embrace Bert's mother, I could feel her anguish. No mother should have to bury her child, regardless of his age. Her love wasn't the same as mine, but every bit as deep and intense. We both knew, without having to find the words, that our hearts would feel a void forever as our everyday thoughts remembered Bert.

I wasn't surprised that the Rosary was attended by such a vast circle of family, relatives, friends, and colleagues. They filled the chapel and spilled out into the foyer. Bert was loved and respected by everyone who knew him. With his heart of gold, there was nothing he wouldn't do to help someone in need. They were eager to pay their respects. Emily and my niece, Regan, had created a collage of pictures representing many happy events in our lives, and so had Bert's sisters. They had spent a great deal of time on them, but I don't remember seeing or appreciating them that evening. Emily and Regan had also made a CD containing some of Bert's favorite music, and it played while people visited before the start of the Rosary. The one song I remember wistfully was "Look At You Girl," written and sung by Chris Ledoux, a former rodeo champion from Wyoming who became a beloved country singer before he died at an early age of cancer. Bert had told me many times the song was written especially for him about me. Bert's nephew, Andrew, played his guitar and sang another song during the service, but at the time, I was sitting with clenched hands, hoping I could hold myself together. I couldn't allow myself to listen to the words.

The Rosary is also known as a Vigil or Wake. Family and friends gather around the dead one to pray for him, to remember his life, and to console each another. Since the service has the very specific purpose of attending to the soul of the dead one, prayers for Bert were said and the priest led us in the Rosary (Glorious Mysteries). The Eternal Rest prayer was prayed after each decade of the Rosary: *Eternal rest grant unto him, O Lord; and let perpetual light shine upon him. May he rest in peace. Amen.*

When the priest asked if anyone wanted to say a few words about Bert, his brothers-in-law, Jay and Eric, rose, as did my brother Pete and my brother-in-law Roy. It took great courage for each of them to do this, as it wasn't in their nature to speak in public at all, let alone in such an emotionally charged atmosphere. They were all very close to Bert. Two of Emily's friends gave short and sweet eulogies recounting how much fun they'd had with Bert during their visits to our home; he always made them laugh.

At the suggestion of one of my sisters, I had written a letter to Bert to be read at the Rosary, but we knew that none of us would be able to do so and get through it coherently. Thankfully, my friend Ana was willing to read my goodbye.

> To my dearest, beloved husband,
> Saying goodbye to you for the last time is the hardest thing I have ever had to do. Words cannot express the void I am feeling in my heart today. It is an unbearable pain; a pain I never knew existed. When our paths first crossed fourteen years ago, we both knew it was in God's plan for us to be together. We overcame many obstacles, but by the grace of God, our love for each other continued to grow. You would always thank me for changing your life, and I would thank you in return for changing mine. Our love was the kind some people never get to experience. We knew we were blessed. Not a day went by that I didn't thank God for bringing you to me.
> Although the love I have had for you is different from others, I have to remember that everyone who knew you has also suffered a huge loss with your death. Our children lost a father, your parents a son, your sisters a brother, your grandmother a grandson, and my parents a son-in-law. Many relatives and friends whose lives have been touched by you will never forget you.
> Thank you, honey, for everything. All you ever wanted for our children and for me was our happiness. Everything you did was for us. You were the most loving, generous, compassionate, and unselfish man I have ever known. To me, you were invincible . . . a man made of steel. There was absolutely nothing you couldn't fix or make better. I now know you were a mere human being, just like all of us here today. But you are a child of God

and were placed in this world as a gift to us. Perhaps — although it is so difficult to accept — God knew you had fulfilled all He wanted you to do here and took you home to be with Him.

Today, I need forgiveness for asking why. I will try to pray that God will give me the courage and strength to go on living . . . not a day at a time, because that seems like an eternity, but a minute at a time.

I have no regrets. We told each other every day of our love. We missed each other while you were so far away during the week at work, but the excitement and anticipation of seeing each other each weekend brought butterflies to my stomach. I have no choice but to go on, but I will not do so without you beside me. As Chris said to me, now we have you with us 100% of the time.

Thank you for loving me in your special way and for opening my heart to accept your love and to experience what it is like to truly love somebody in return. I am blessed with many good memories and I will cherish them for the rest of my life. The love we shared can never be taken away from me.

May you rest in peace, my dear husband. I will always feel your presence along with God's. I'm sure you are delighted to be reunited with Gramps. We will all be together again one day, as that is part of God's perfect and divine plan.

Your loving wife always, Letty

I cried that night until I was exhausted from the effort. Then I took another sleeping pill to escape reality. I told myself sleep was necessary so that I could drag myself from bed the next morning and attend the funeral. There would be so many people there. Their eyes would be watching me. They'd be wondering what I was thinking and how I was handling the tragic event. They'd be asking themselves *why?* just as I was. They'd never ask me, but they'd ask each other, hoping someone would have an explanation. A few would want to know for gossip reasons. It was to be expected. Right then, the *why* wasn't important to me. I was more concerned about the *how*: how would I get through the day without collapsing in public?

I had prayed the rosary, but my heart wasn't in it. Other thoughts intruded upon my ability to worship and believe. Where was God in my time of trouble? Why wasn't He making me feel better? How could I sit in church and sing praises to Him while I suffered and relived over and over again the brutal death of my beloved husband and thought of the anguish he was in during that split second of time? Where was God when Bert needed Him? I had never felt so alone, even with family and friends in close attendance. *Why, God? Why Bert? Why me?* I felt like Job's wife, who urged him to renounce God for the severity of his unearned punishment.

Bert's son, Bert Michael, had not arrived from Mexico yet, but he and his mother would be at the funeral with his grandparents. My heart ached for him. He was just sixteen years old and saw his father only a couple of times each year. Fortunately, they enjoyed a close and loving father-son relationship, and whenever he came to visit, it was as though no time had elapsed since he last stayed with us. The school year was almost over. It was about time for his summer visit. This wasn't what he had anticipated. He would be stoic, but inside, he'd be a bundle of nerves. He might even be angry, like I was. Confused, like I was. In denial, like I was. As long as we didn't see the coffin, we could pretend we were merely participants in a drama. But always, in the back of our silent grieving, reality lurked.

Bert Michael's father was dead.

My husband was dead.

Once again, my sisters were in the house to assist with our parents, Christopher and Emily, and me. With their help, I managed to pull myself together and once again dressed in black — the color of mourning. Black showed dignity and respect for the family. This was especially important to older Latinos. Modest black attire sent an unspoken message to other attendees. It communicated that I was soberly reflecting on the life of the deceased one. My husband. I was just going through the motions and not "present" in the moment. Someone took my elbow and steered me out of the house and into a car.

As soon as we arrived at the church, the family gathered for the traditional walk down the aisle to the front pews. I saw Bert Michael with his mother. He resembled his father in so many ways. I reached out to him, and when I held him close, his tall slender body seemed lifeless. Like the rest of us, he was in a world somewhere far away.

Before I could take one step to enter the church, I wrapped my arms around the casket, as though I were hugging Bert one last time. I had not been able to view his body before the Rosary. No one had. I imagined him as he had been that last Tuesday morning in our bedroom, handsome and strong. With my face buried in the softness of the flower petals, my tears watered them. Someone tugged on my arm and drew me away so the procession could begin.

The pallbearers were all Bert's brother in-laws from both sides of our families and his best friend, Noe. They carried his casket slowly down the church aisle, following the priest. As we walked immediately behind them, I watched as the casket was placed before the altar. My eyes took in the beautiful floral display draped over the top and the sombrero that had been added at the suggestion of his mother and sisters. I felt my knees buckling under me. The lump in my throat grew and my heart thudded against my chest wall. While sitting through the service, it occurred to me that I had not gone anywhere near the casket at the Rosary. A wave of guilt washed over me. What was I thinking? Why hadn't someone reminded me? As my eyes stared sightlessly at the priest and each person taking part in the service, my thoughts drifted time and again to the Rosary service. No matter how hard I tried, I couldn't remember any details. I couldn't remember the music, the words spoken by the men in our family, or the collages made by the women. My mind was a blank screen.

In a perpetual daze, I vaguely heard the music being played during the service and moved my lips during a couple of the hymns, which were the standard ones sung at most Catholic funerals. Nothing I had chosen. Surely, I wasn't the exception. Few mourners are able to think of the details of the service when they are in such a state of numbness. After the

21

priest had intoned the Liturgy of the Word, which included Bible sermons, a homily and a Psalm, he went on to the Liturgy of the Eucharist, a Eucharist prayer, and then Holy Communion. The service included readings by several of Bert's nieces and nephews. Unfortunately, I don't remember any of this in detail. At the time, it was as though I were watching a 1930's silent movie on television.

The service ended and I joined other family members in following the casket back down the aisle and out to the waiting hearse. Someone led me to a vehicle. I took my seat and stared out the window as we drove slowly to the Mission Park South burial grounds. This was the last stop. Soon, it would be over. Walking across the grass to the gravesite, I had my arm tucked into that of my son. I felt his tenseness and knew the death and burial of a loved one was a life occurrence he wasn't ready to experience. Finally, his feelings burst out of him in a sort of desperation. "I can't take this, Mom! I can't hold it in any longer. *I don't know what to do.*"

Squeezing his hand, I whispered. "It's okay, son. It's okay to cry. You don't have to hold it in." I wanted him to cry. It was important for him to let go and allow himself to grieve openly. Trembling and not wanting to let the crack in his wall of pain expand, he let the tears welling in his eyes spill down his cheeks, and then the crack burst open and he couldn't stop the flow. For that moment in time, I was able to climb out of my dark pit and mother him.

I was led to a chair under a white canopy. Emily, Christopher, and Bert Michael sat beside me. Members from both families sat in chairs behind us. The Rite of Committal at the graveside includes prayers, and I bit my lip to quell the quivering. The priest made the Sign of the Cross over the casket and then brought me the cross that had been on the casket. I clutched it tightly and heard the final prayer: *Eternal rest grant unto him, O Lord. And let perpetual light shine upon him. May he rest in peace. Amen. May his soul and the souls of all the faithful departed, through the mercy of God, rest in peace. Amen.*

My house was filled with family and friends the rest of the day and into the night following the funeral. Because of their thoughtfulness and generosity, there was more than enough food and drinks for the two meals and snacks. They also brought donations for the cost of the funeral, flowers, and other things that were so welcoming. I was deeply grateful for their presence and dreaded the moment the house would be empty of their voices, as they shared happy memories of their relationship with Bert and laughed over humorous situations. Bert's family and their friends had a similar gathering at his parents' home.

At one point of the evening, as we stood in the darkness and stared up at the night sky, I asked my brother Pete something that had been on my mind since Wednesday morning. "If Bert took his life, Pete, does that mean he isn't in heaven? We've always been taught that only God can take a life . . . when He's ready for us to leave this earth. No one has said anything to me. I can't find any peace of mind, if —"

"Listen, Letty, if Bert took his life, he was in such mental pain, he wasn't in his right mind. At that moment, he wasn't thinking rationally. He couldn't. God forgives believers, even when they make such a dire decision in their last moment of life."

I sighed in relief. Even in my grief of the moment and my anger at God for not making His presence known to me and to Bert at the time, I remembered John 3:16: *For God so loved the world that he gave his one and only Son, that whoever believes in him, shall not perish, but have eternal life.* Bert believed. Christ's death on the cross was meant to forgive all the sins of the believer, even those that were forgotten or not remembered and confessed . . . even the sin of suicide when a believer was not in his right mind. Bert was in heaven with God and suffering no more. He had lived a good Christian life and was a loving and supportive husband, father, son, brother, and friend. While that gave me a modicum of comfort in my mind, I didn't feel comforted in my soul. I was a long way from finding my way back to a strong faith. I could mouth the prayers and hope, but I still felt angry and defeated and even doubted there was a God.

*How long, O Lord? Will You forget me forever? How long
will You hide Your face from me? How long shall I take
counsel in my soul, having sorrow in my heart all the day?*
— Psalm 13:1-2

Chapter 3

Signs of Hope

Grieving the death of a loved one doesn't end with the funeral service. During the first couple of weeks, I felt as though I were dying myself. Mine was a slower, more lingering death caused by the breaking of my heart and the bleeding of my soul. I wanted to stay in my bedroom with the door closed, but I had my parents to think about and, most of all, my children. I didn't want to face any of them or engage in conversation, but I made the effort each day, creeping about the house, only speaking when spoken to and sending the silent message that I didn't want to be there.

Sonya came daily to tend to the needs of my parents, who were unable to handle their own needs, let alone take on mine. In addition, she cooked meals for all of us and washed clothes and did sundry tasks way beyond her job description. She didn't need to be asked. She simply tended to whatever needed to be done out of love and her innate sense of caring.

My ACTS (Adoration, Community, Theology, and Service) sisters from church brought food to the house every day for the first three weeks. The growth of our friendships during this time of continuous stress was and has been a sustaining grace for me. Still, I was not good company or wholly appreciative of their sincere concern. Words of sympathy and encouragement were always welcomed, but they were like Band-Aids on a deep and gaping wound . . . only temporary fixes, easily peeled off, and inadequate for covering the incessant festering that kept my heart oozing pain.

Christopher was on edge, visibly irritated, and more than a little annoyed over Bert's decision and my reaction to it. Even if I had insisted he sit down and discuss his feelings with me, he would have declined and withdrawn into himself. He was grieving in his own way and seemed to find personal comfort by hanging out with his friends, pretending nothing extraordinary had happened. Sadly, he also tried to drown his feelings with an overindulgence in alcohol, hoping this would numb his pain. I knew this was destructive and risky behavior, but again, I took no strong measures to stop it. Who was I to advise family members about what they should do to lessen or at least deal with their inner confusion? Truthfully, I think I was subconsciously concerned he was blaming me for Bert's suicide. It seemed logical. I was blaming myself, too. I should have been more observant of behavior changes in Bert. I should have asked more questions and taken a stronger interest in our financial situation.

Emily was in her own kind of denial, one that is typical of teenagers, but exacerbated by the violence that makes a suicide wholly different from even death by car accident. She insisted on returning to school the day after the funeral and kept busy with her end-of-year school activities, preparing for and taking exams and making tentative plans for the summer. She attended various functions with her friends and stayed in her room when she was home. We passed each other in the house like proverbial two ships at night in a vast sea. I saw what I wanted to see and told myself both children seemed to be doing all right. They were young and would "get over it" in time. That's what I wanted to believe, because then I wouldn't have to do anything or feel guilty for my passivity.

I vaguely remembered a line from Arthur Miller's play *After the Fall*. He wrote the play after his divorce from Marilyn Monroe and after her suicide by an overdose of drugs. People said the play was about his own life and relationships. One line was quoted continuously, about a suicide actually killing two people.

In no way did I believe that Bert killed himself because of anything I had done, but, nevertheless, the thought intruded on all the other possible reasons concocted by my grappling mind. I needed a reason.

During the week following the funeral, time seemed to move in slow motion. My sisters and brother came to the house daily to help with paperwork and decisions. Bert had not written a will. We had to consult an attorney about what to do. I was bombarded with questions, questions, questions, and I was expected to come up with answers. This was my life. No one else's. These were now my bills. Without an income, how would they be paid? What was the status of our bank account? What about the mortgage and insurance and cars? What about Bert's truck? Was there a life insurance policy? Too late, I learned that loving someone doesn't mean you can bury your head in the sand and allow that person to take over your life. I should have taken a more active role in our business affairs. I should have insisted upon our both writing wills, after our marriage. I should have . . . .

I hadn't. Now, under the strain and stress produced by my profound grief, I had to become a business woman. Life goes on for the living. A cliché, but reality. There are laws to take into consideration and company rules and regulations to follow. A survivor of suicide is not exempt from any of them. And so little by little, day by day, I walked through the tasks that needed my immediate attention. I wrote to-do lists and stared at them with vacant eyes, wishing I could wave a magic wand to produce a genie to take care of them for me. I resented having to deal with the endless financial issues. They kept me awake at night. I found myself becoming increasingly angry at Bert for putting me in this position. What was he thinking? Clearly, he wasn't! Deeply in debt, he had became clinically depressed and saw no hope for a future. He masked his depression from me and made no mention of our financial straits. It was the *macho* thing to do. To "lose face" in the eyes of a spouse, family members or friends was frowned upon by Latino men.

After admitting my frustration and anger to myself, a wave of guilt would wash over me and I'd cry myself to sleep. I needed Bert's help. I needed to discuss every issue with him. I wished he'd walk into the house and say it was all a nightmare. Then I imagined all the things he could do from heaven to show me he was at least with me in spirit. If he was, indeed, able to see the kids and me, then I wanted a sign he was watching out for us and that he cared about our suffering.

One day, I noticed a male cardinal in all its red splendor perched high on a tree branch near the patio. It burst into its unique sweet and melodic song, repeating it several times. *purdy, purdy, purdy . . . whoit, whoit, whoit, whoit . . . what-cheer, what-cheer . . .wheet, wheet, wheet, wheet.* Since cardinals don't migrate, it had probably been visiting our yard for a long time and I hadn't paid much attention. Then his song changed. More like *chip, chip, chip.* Was he warning the female and their nestlings of danger? Could his visit at this very moment be a symbol of Bert's presence? Was Bert watching out for his own "nestlings" and for me? From that moment on, I noticed the cardinal on almost a daily basis, appreciating his attentiveness to his family.

The cardinal's presence at one of my low moments got me to thinking about other "happenings" that I chose to believe were Bert's way of making his presence known to me. The evening of the funeral, for instance, I had gone to Bert's chest of drawers to put away a pair of socks. As I opened the drawer, I started to cry. "Bert, why did you choose to leave me?" I wailed. I closed the drawer and turned to glance toward our bed. Knowing he would never share it with me again brought a crushing heaviness in my chest. At that very instant, I glanced at the television set, which I had left on to have a "voice" of another human in the room and to interrupt my wildly fluctuating thoughts. The movie of *Casper the Ghost* was showing. I had never seen the movie before and was fascinated by the sight of the unhappy and seemingly lonely young girl lying on her bed and talking to someone who wasn't with her, and Casper appeared and promised to always be there with her. As she went to sleep, Casper laid gently beside her on the bed. Instantly, I felt chills run up my spine. Was this a sign from Bert? I choose to believe it was. He wanted me to know that while he wouldn't be with me in body, he would always be by my side in spirit.

A week later, one of my tasks was to get a state-required inspection sticker for my car. When I arrived at the station, the man in charge said he was unable to authorize the new sticker, as one of my car's taillights wasn't working and he didn't have a replacement bulb to fit my model car. He provided the name of another inspection site right up the street and recommended I try there. I did as he suggested. This inspector was unusually nice and polite. He replaced the bulb in the taillight, checked the tires, windshield wipers, under the hood, and the brakes. Then he placed the new inspection sticker on the windshield. "Thank you so much," I said. "How much do I owe you?"

His eyes met mine. "Don't worry about it," he said.

Tears trickled down my cheeks. I saw his confused look through a watery blur. "My . . . my husband just d-died," I stuttered. "I . . . I think I just felt his presence."

"I'm sorry," the man muttered. "Things have been difficult for me, too. My son is very ill and he's getting treatments in Houston."

Immediately, I felt a connection. Perhaps he had seen how troubled and in pain I was and had made an effort to assuage his own suffering. Regardless of why or how this incident happened, I believe Bert had something to do with it. Bert would have done the same thing for another woman in my condition and he was letting me know my needs would be taken care of one at a time.

The next morning, after dropping Emily off at school, I drove down the highway crying. The tears still came and went at will, without my conscious consent. I indulged in another pity party and groaned aloud at Bert, fighting my fury at being left to deal with so many tasks and feeling totally inept and helpless. I glanced at a church that was being remodeled and noticed a huge banner with bold text that said MAKING A ROOM FOR YOU. I had no idea how long the sign had been there. I traveled the road every day and had never seen it before now. Was it another message meant specifically for me?

One evening, after everyone had left the house, I sat on a chair on our front porch thinking about how much I missed Bert and wishing he could miraculously come home. Unexpectedly and seemingly out of nowhere, a light breeze stirred the wind chimes hanging nearby. Startled, I turned toward them. Bert had given me the angel chimes several years ago. Was he telling me he was with the angels in heaven singing praises to his loving God?

My heart hardened. Where was this loving God when Bert needed Him? Where was He now, when I needed Him? I didn't feel His presence or hear His voice.

Early one morning, I walked out onto the patio with my breakfast coffee. A doe with her tiny fawn stared at me for several seconds and then turned and walked slowly toward the creek in back of our property. The fawn was still wobbly and trying hard to walk beside her. The doe left her near the creek to go find food. She would return, but the fawn looked around, as though fearful and lonely. I immediately thought of Bert. Was he telling me not to worry or be afraid. That I would learn to walk without him and soon be loping through my daily tasks?

Another morning, I was just about to open my eyes when I felt someone rubbing my arm. I thought Sonya or Emily had come into my room to wake me up. I caught a glimpse of what appeared to be the shadow of an arm. But, no one was in my bedroom. I believe it was Bert. He often rubbed my arm in just such a way.

Of course I wondered if these incidents were merely a figment of my imagination and the result of the shock I was still experiencing. But, at the time, they were very real to me. Signs, messages, coincidences . . . whatever they are called, I felt and saw them. They were signs of hope.

*We know that suffering produces perseverance;
perseverance, character; and character, hope. And hope
does not disappoint us, because God has poured out his
love into our hearts by the Holy Spirit. —* Romans 5:3-5
(NIV)

Chapter 4

Breaking the Barrier of Silence

Even by the end of the third week, I was struggling to make it through the day. I couldn't see beyond the moment. I went through the motions of getting dressed, greeting my parents, and talking with Sonya about their meals. Food held no interest for me. "I don't know. What do you think?" were my standard replies to any questions put to me. To think too far ahead caused increased anxiety. I was consumed with thoughts of how I could manage to live the rest of my life without Bert. Life held less meaning without my partner.

My family and friends reminded me continuously of all the things I had to live for. First and foremost were my children. Their ability to finish the school year, and their future achievements and capacity to find contentment and happiness would depend a great deal on my heartfelt caring, positive input, genuine interest, and continual support. They had loved Bert, too, and in a finger snap he was gone from their lives, just like from mine. The concept of instant death was far more difficult for young people to comprehend than it was for an adult who had a decade or more experience with the vagaries of life, especially when someone they knew and loved had lost his life at his own hand.

Rationally, I knew my two children needed me and deserved to know I would never purposely make their survival worse by taking my own life. They had heard me declare over and again how my life was no longer worth living and that I wanted to die. Horrible words to hear from a mother's lips. Despite knowing this, I was in deep denial and shock and utterly incapable of thinking rationally. I felt helpless to do anything other than mourn my personal loss.

I had put off dealing with the bills and mail that had accumulated during these first three weeks as a widow. The envelopes were scattered on my desk. Sorting through them, checking my bank account, and having to take action seemed too difficult to handle. Although I had been in charge of paying the household bills, I had never enjoyed the task. I had quit working several years back as my children got older and my parents became less able to live independently. I had also wanted to spend more time with Bert at the ranch. With his encouragement, I had ended my childcare business, which I had run out of my home for the previous thirteen years. I was grateful for the opportunity to do this and enjoyed my newfound freedom.

Although our new financial situation had made it difficult to make ends meet on occasion, it was stable most of the time. Bert had become more anxious with the added burden of being the sole breadwinner, but he hadn't wanted me to worry about it. I learned, later, that he was in a bigger financial mess than I had ever imagined.

At my brother Pete's insistence and with his help, I learned I had enough money to pay the immediate bills, so for the time being I wouldn't need to add job hunting to the list of things that was already keeping my stress level elevated. I would, however, need to find ways to cut expenses in order to pay for what was absolutely necessary for survival. Pete and my brother-in-law Jay stepped up to help me with the more legal financial issues, tax, car and home insurance issues, and work-related matters, such as reporting Bert's death to Social Security. And, of course, since Bert had died intestate (without a legal will), there were regulations to follow in Texas regarding our assets to determine what was considered separate or community property. Each ruling was riddled with exceptions. This matter was turned over to an attorney.

Halfheartedly, I started to write thank you notes to those who had sent flowers and supported me in sundry ways during this very trying time. My heart was overflowing with gratitude, but writing the words and thinking about what was behind them became increasingly difficult. I knew this would be a project I could only work on for a short time each day. The task caused an emotional upheaval that completely drained me of what little energy I had. Again, my sisters stepped in and assured me no one would expect an immediate expression of my appreciation. So the thank you cards became another project I set aside.

Everything that caught my eye and every place I went reminded me of Bert. From the moment I woke up in the morning and had my first cup of coffee, I would think of him. Over the years of our marriage, I had often asked, "Why does your coffee always taste so good?"

"Mamas," he'd say, "it's my secret measurements." If he didn't call me honey, he'd call me *mamas*. Sometimes, when I'd tell him I loved him, he'd say "mamas" back and I knew he meant "I love you, too." I missed hearing that endearment. I'd never hear it again from his lips.

One of the most difficult early decisions I had to make, to ensure I could sustain a reasonable living for the kids and me, was to sell Bert's boat. I hated having to do it. Years ago, he had bought a Jon boat (sometimes called a johnboat) — a flat-bottomed craft with a couple of bench seats that made it suitable for duck hunting or fishing because of the greater level of stability. Over time, he sold it and then bought a slightly larger boat, until he finally got his keeper. Fishing was his passion. "Letty," he'd say, "when I'm in the middle of the Aransas Bay, with no one around as I watch the sun rise, I am so at peace. Fishing is a religious experience for me." It was his special time with God. Needless to say, selling his boat was difficult for me. For Christopher, too. It was like selling a piece of Bert's soul. But the money paid more bills.

The process brought to mind many memories of our trips to Rockport, on the east coast of Texas and only a couple of hours' drive from San Antonio. Bert knew exactly which weeks of particular months were best for speckled trout, redfish, flounder and black drum fish. Sometimes I'd go along in the boat with him, but more often he'd go alone in the early morning hours and I'd stay behind and write or just enjoy shelling and walking along the shoreline. Bert and I both preferred being alone together or with the kids, rather than attending parties or being around large groups.

An idea had been in the back of my mind and now I made the firm decision. I would drive to Rockport and spend a few days alone. I knew it would be hard to do, but I wanted to feel Bert's presence and Rockport was the best possible place to do this. I wasn't ready to go to the ranch. We had always stayed at the same place, a small hotel with a cottage look — light blue with white trim, a big front porch, and balconies with comfortable white rocking chairs, and a view that overlooked the ever-changing vista of the Bay.

The night before I planned to leave, my sister Elsa called me. Apparently, she had been made the designated caller on behalf of all my sisters. "Letty," she said, "we're very concerned about your driving to Rockport by yourself. You're not in a good emotional place yet. Don't you think it's a little too soon for making such a trip? What possible good can it do you?"

I knew what she was implying — that maybe I'd never come home — and I wasn't in the mood to argue with her or anyone else in my family. "I'll think about it," I said. "Maybe you're right." As soon a I hung up the phone, I continued with my packing. I had to do what I had to do. Waiting would only prolong my stagnant state of mind. My sisters were worried about me, and I understood their concern. But I couldn't listen to them. Wouldn't listen. This was the first individual decision I had made as a widow, without advice. I wasn't listening to myself either. Christopher and Emily were on summer vacation and had activities planned with their friends. Sonya and my parents would be fine in our house for a while without me.

The next morning I left for Rockport with my Bible, meditation CDs, pen, journal, and notebook computer. I was ready to grieve in private, and I hoped to come to terms with God.

Upon arriving, I felt utterly alone. I had nothing but my thoughts to keep me company, and I wasn't at all prepared for the crushing weight of my suffering. I had finally accepted that Bert was dead. He would not be coming back to me. My mind was no longer protecting me from facing that truth. I could not minimize the consequences of his action. Without the protection of my denial, I felt more vulnerable to everything that threatened a sense of control over my life. Where would I get the money to make car, mortgage, and utility payments? How could I meet Christopher's growing college expenses? How could I be the mother I wanted to be to my children, when I couldn't even find the energy to get dressed in the morning? How long would it take me to process all the ramifications of this shocking blow and come to grips with the endless challenges that lay ahead of me?

The truth is that at that moment in time, the desire to go on living wasn't in me. I saw nothing good in my future, only pure drudgery, endless misery, and devastating loneliness. A rush of breath-snatching fear overwhelmed me and I spent the first few hours crying until I was physically and mentally exhausted. I was a failure. I was useless as a mother and a daughter, and I wouldn't blame my sisters and Pete if they never darkened my doorstep again. How could I take care of my parents and my children when I couldn't even take care of myself?

Again, my anger at Bert grew and right beside it my anger with God. I had trusted them both. I had believed they loved me and would always make decisions that were in my best interest. In the best interest of my family. Both had let me down. What did I have to believe in now? I was in a deep pit of despair and I could no longer count on either to pull me out.

For the next full day, I replayed everything I could remember about the weeks preceding the suicide. What had I missed? What hadn't I seen that could have put a stop to the madness? What was wrong with my relationship with Bert that he felt he couldn't confide in me? Did he see me as weak minded, too emotional, too much a worrywart to deal with the truth? Did he think I wouldn't go along with changing our lifestyle to lessen his stress over financial matters? That I'd find him less desirable or less manly . . . less the dependable breadwinner? Why hadn't he told me how he was feeling? What if I had said something different the last time we spoke with each other? Or what if I had driven to Laredo with him that Tuesday morning, as I sometimes did? Had he already planned his suicide, or was it something he decided at the spur of the moment after receiving news about our financial difficulties? Exactly what had triggered his final decision? Had he been afraid? Had he prayed?

I knew Bert loved Bert Michael and my two children and me as much as humanly possible. Had he ended his life *because* he loved us so much and thought we'd be better off without him? Surely he had known how devastating his choice would be for us. Yet he had abandoned us. And he did it with no explanation whatsoever. No note. No final word. Just silence.

The *whys, what ifs,* and *if onlys* chased each other through my mind for hours on end. How did other people survive a tragedy like this? Although I knew that each year thousands of others were left behind to endure the same trauma I was experiencing, I was in such a dark tunnel of grief, I saw no consolation in statistics. Other people weren't me. Statistics didn't bring comfort or provide answers to my questions. I wanted rational answers for the irrational action of my husband. I had been told by family and friends for three weeks that things would get better with time and that Bert had not been in his right mind when he picked up his gun. I believed that, but I wanted and needed more than statements of solace or tidbits of logical explanation. What did they know about what I was going through? I could not visualize a better tomorrow.

And so I cried and cried some more. At times, my tears would simply roll unbidden down my cheeks in effortless rivulets and I'd brush them away with the back of my hand. Other times, I would erupt into a frightening outburst of sobs that produced enough water to overflow a concrete dam. The voluminous expulsion of tears and sobs was so uncontrollable, I was certain I'd never be able to stop it. The sounds coming from my throat frightened me.

Again, I wondered where God was when I needed Him. I had always prayed for my husband's safety. Hadn't God heard me? Had He decided I wasn't a good enough Christian to have my prayers answered? Had I committed some unforgiveable sin that had broken my relationship with Him? I dived headfirst into extreme wretchedness, feeling exactly like Job when God allowed Satan to test his faith and Satan took away everything Job had ever valued, including his children, his cattle, and business, and money. Everything. Job's friends came to lament over his misery with him, finally telling him he must have committed some great sin or God would never allow such a monumental catastrophe. Job tried to think of such a sin and came up with none. He pleaded with God. *"How many wrongs and sins have I committed? Show me my offense and my sin. Why do you hide your face and consider me your enemy?"*

Yes, I felt like Job, but at that moment, I lacked Job's fortitude. I hated the way I felt. I screamed aloud, "I don't want to do this!" I wanted to crawl out of my own skin and run away. But where would I go? No matter where or how far I went, the pain of reality followed me. Somehow, I would have to come to grips with my agony and rise above it. But how? I was experiencing total body and mind paralysis. Before I could do anything, I determined, I'd have to go ahead and feel the full depth and harshness of my grief. Avoiding it, denying it, or rushing through it would only prolong it or bring it back later.

I finally fell on my knees with my hands pressed against my heart and begged God to help me. Like Job, I wished I had never been born, because then I wouldn't have to suffer. God reminded me that Job, despite his far worse tribulations, had never lost his faith. Question it, yes. Demand an answer. Yes. Plead for wisdom to understand the answer. Yes. Job just wanted to know why. He *needed* to know why. So did I. "Please, God, help me accept what is going on in my life right now. I don't understand any of this. Like Job, I am traveling blind. Bert's suicide is a mystery that seems to have no acceptable answer."

Most of the time I spent in Rockport consisted of attempting to pray, reading my Bible for any verses that might bring me some sort of comfort, journaling, and searching the Internet to find anything on the subject of suicide that might be helpful, all the while reflecting on the vacillating emotions that were tearing me apart.

After a couple of days in solitude, my friend De called and said she was coming to console me with her presence. The evening she arrived, she informed me she planned to meet her brother and sister-in-law for dinner at a restaurant across the street from my hotel. They lived in the area and wanted both of us to join them. It took some persuasion, but I agreed to go along.

I mostly listened to their quiet conversation. They carefully avoided the subject of suicide and asked me no questions other than how I was doing. "As well as can be expected," I said. We ordered our dinners and I tried to muster up interest, but food still held no interest for me. The evening seemed to be going reasonably well when, totally out of the blue, I was hit with the full force of my grief. *Again.* Hearing the measured voice of De's brother brought it all back. Bert would never sit across the table from me again. We'd never share dinner in a Rockport restaurant. I was not like other widows. I couldn't talk about how brave my husband had been while dealing with cancer or heart failure. I was fully aware of and felt the pity of my hosts. I heard their unasked questions.

Quickly, I excused myself and dashed out of the restaurant. As I stumbled across the street to the hotel, I could feel the floodtide of emotions building rapidly inside me. I hurried across the lobby and headed directly to my room. As soon as I opened the door, the huge lump in my throat dislodged and I fell prostate onto the bed, sobbing for what seemed like hours. It was as though I had just received the news of Bert's death. The pain was as raw as it had been those first few hours of that unforgettable day.

When my tears finally subsided, I was physically exhausted, drained of every ounce of energy. I decided that if I intended to do anything outside my home of a social nature in the near future, I would need a game plan, including an emergency exit and something to say before using it. I clearly had no control over my emotions yet and could expect such unpredictable upheavals to happen again.

Early on the day of my departure, I was sitting on the balcony outside my room facing the Bay. I realized it had been exactly one month since Bert had taken his life. Somehow, I had survived without him for thirty days, hour by hour, minute by minute. I also realized that I had subconsciously believed Bert was simply out on his boat and would enter the hotel room at any moment. I wanted this to happen so much, I had convinced myself that by simply being in a place we had both enjoyed, my nightmare would come to an end and my life would take up where it had left off a month ago.

This was an eye-opener for me. Perhaps the trip had served its purpose after all. I had needed to mourn in private, without the eyes and ears of my family members judging my stability and sanity. I had needed to end my state of denial and accept the truth. I was a widow. I was a single mother of two children. My new life had begun. Bert would no longer be a part of it.

Back at home again, I started to do little things around the house, mostly to stay busy and keep my mind off Bert. I had done nothing to remove his presence from the house. His personal belongings were exactly where they had always been. I hadn't wanted to disturb anything, initially believing he would return. Now, I felt a degree of comfort in seeing his clothes in the closet, his toothbrush near the bathroom sink, the book he had been reading on the table next to our bed. I had no intention of getting rid of anything anytime soon.

On any given day, at any given time, I would know what Bert would be doing if he were still with us. I couldn't seem to scrub such thoughts from my mind. They were incessant and palpable. In any situation, I knew what he would say or do. It was hard to find a new "normal" in my daily routine, when my mind was so determined to keep me stuck in the past.

It wasn't long before friends and family had to return to their personal routines. Their families needed them and their individual priorities had to take precedence over mine. As the house emptied, I felt more alone, especially at night. It was difficult to sleep without the security of Bert's sweatshirt. I'd hold it close to me, like a child with a special blanket, and pray that he'd visit me in my dreams. I wanted to know he was okay and happy . . . and that he still loved me. Even while I prayed for such a blessing, I'd fight against my resentment that he hadn't left me a note to treasure forever. How could he love me as much as he had proclaimed and then leave me without a single word of explanation or assurance? He could have left it at the ranch or in his truck, if he hadn't wanted me to accidently find it at home.

Still, I struggled to accept that a normally rational and sane person does not suddenly take his life. He was sick. He was clinically depressed, and people in that condition do not have the capacity to think logically. I was having the same trouble. Surely, I should be able to understand. And forgive. I knew, however, that I would be haunted by this life-shattering event forever and it would leave me feeling less than whole for the rest of my life.

Now that I had climbed further out of my personal crater of heartache, I became more aware of my children's suffering. Although I could tell that Christopher was struggling, he remained stoic. Emily acted as though nothing tragic had occurred in her life and to our family unit. I realized she had rarely cried since that first day. Bits and pieces of what I had read on the Internet while in Rockport came to mind. Adults grieve in different ways and so do young people and children. Some internalize their feelings and have difficulty in expressing them. They think they look different from their friends and everyone is staring at them and gossiping about the tragedy. They think some are purposely avoiding them, as though they are dangerous to be around; like they're a criminal. A murderer. They feel ashamed by the action of their loved one.

In my moments of lucidity, I had reasoned my kids needed their "space." They'd come to me when they were ready. I was deceiving myself, of course. Why would they seek comfort from me, when I was such a mess myself? I had hoped that maybe they were waiting for me to become a little stronger and would be ready now if I approached them. We needed to comfort each other. But I left my reaching out to a mere, "How are you doing?" When they said, "Okay," I let it go and then dealt with my own guilt and shame for being such a failure as a mother.

My brother-in-law, Roy, had asked me several times what I planned to do about Bert's truck . . . the one he had driven to Laredo. He had driven it back to San Antonio and parked it in the junkyard of my brother-in-law Dain, waiting until I was ready to make a decision. After some discussion about our options, I decided I couldn't keep up with the payments on a vehicle that would merely sit in the driveway. Christopher agreed, but we had both been dreading the day of reckoning. Our plan was for him to pick it up, bring it home, and then the two of us would head straight over to the bank and turn it in. I gathered all the papers, including the registration. Before we left the house, I looked at my son to see how he was handling this difficult task. "Is there any doubt in your mind that you might want to keep Bert's truck and sell yours instead?" I could tell by his silence that he wasn't quite sure. I hugged him. "We won't make a decision today then. I'll make this month's payment and we'll think about it." He was visibly relieved. I could tell he had been crying in the truck while driving home to pick me up. It had been very difficult for him to sit behind the wheel in Bert's position. Everything in the vehicle reminded him of his stepfather.

Later that day, I asked my sister Lisa if she would be willing to talk with Christopher to see how he was really doing. The two had a close aunt/nephew relationship. Lisa agreed. Fortunately, he opened up to her and admitted he wasn't doing well at all. He was experiencing alternate feelings of guilt and anger and embarrassment, and he was having terrible nightmares. He couldn't concentrate on anything and he felt restless. He wanted to look forward to going away to college in the fall, but felt guilty for wanting to get away from the house. He thought I'd see it as another abandonment. He was tired of acting like everything was okay, when it wasn't. He had been trying to be strong for me.

Lisa assured him that everyone in the family was feeling the same way. It was normal, under the circumstances. No one wanted to answer questions from strangers and no one wanted to say Bert had killed himself. We all preferred to say he'd had a "heart" attack. He had nothing to feel guilty about. Bert's decision was his own. No one needed to take responsibility.

A couple of days later, I tried to whittle through Emily's wall of silence. "Honey, I know you've been concerned about me this past month. I haven't been myself. None of us have been. We've been handed a mind-crushing blow we never expected to receive. I see you go about your life as though this tragedy hasn't had an effect on you, but I know better. Are you having trouble expressing your feelings?"

"I do get sad," she said. "Really sad, but I cry in my head, and I just try to think of the good times."

"It's okay to cry out loud," I said. "I know my buckets of tears have been upsetting and scary for you to witness. I haven't handled this well at all. I'm still not okay and I don't know if I will ever be my old self again. It's very likely you won't be either, but we can learn to enjoy life again, in time. Especially if we help each other. Please don't let your feelings remain trapped in your body. You don't want them to erupt in other more unacceptable ways. I haven't been a good example for you. Taking sleeping pills doesn't make the pain go away. They just put off for a day or two what I have to deal with later in order to heal. I don't want you and Christopher to think drinking or drugs or running yourselves ragged at parties will make your pain go away. They won't."

I had made a decision to find professional help for both of them, either a support group or some sort of counseling. My sister Laura approached me one day. "I've been doing some research," she said. "I've found a local support group for suicide survivors. I think you should attend one of their meetings, Letty. I'll take you, if you don't want to go alone. The people in such a group are just like you. They know how you feel and it will be a safe environment where you can express yourself without embarrassment. Maybe it will bring you some of the comfort none of us have been able to provide for you."

I agreed to attend the meeting. I had read about support groups on the Internet, while in Rockport. I was more than a little nervous and hesitant to speak to anyone after I arrived at the meeting and found a seat. Several minutes passed and I listened quietly to the survival stories of others. Some had suffered symptoms like mine for months, some for literally years. That surprised me, but at the same time, it validated my belief that my life was always going to be affected by what Bert had done. I wondered if I would ever really get better. A man told about his son's death, after jumping from the window of a three-story building. A woman told of the death of her daughter due to an overdose of prescription medications. Another woman told of how her father had killed himself three weeks after his wife had died of cancer. There were others, equally tragic.

Finally, already in tears, I had the urge to speak. I told about my initial and lingering shock to learn my husband had shot himself in the head, about my inability to concentrate on anything, to make decisions about even insignificant things, and to do anything useful, especially for my children. Sobbing, I questioned why someone like my husband would choose to end his suffering by causing suffering for his family if he really loved us as he had proclaimed so many times. Another survivor took my hand and gently told me that when Bert took his life, it had nothing to do with the people he loved and who loved him. It was an act of desperation, due to a mental pain so acute nothing else clouded his thinking except ending it. His suffering was likely based upon some terrifying fear of a future he could not face or resolve.

I decided to make an appointment with the therapist who had been highly recommended by my sister-in-law for Christopher and Emily and myself. Although I had been able to speak before those in the support group, a part of me was nervous about sharing my feelings with a professional therapist who was also a stranger, and a part of me was eager to begin some sort of healing process. I was tired of the crying jags and of the sense I couldn't live one more day with the pain.

Christopher had seen the therapist the previous week. When he came home, I asked him how the session had gone. "Mom," he said, "I feel worse now than before I went. It's as if it happened all over again, today."

"Maybe that's where you need to start, Chris. Please don't give up. Go back a few more times and see if talking with an objective listener doesn't help you work out answers to all the questions that haunt you. She'll put things into perspective. Don't hold back. Share all your thoughts and concerns. What you say doesn't go any further than her office. I'll do the same."

Emily went for her first therapy session, although she was apprehensive about sharing her thoughts with a stranger. She was afraid of breaking down, of losing the control she had been so careful to cultivate since the day of the tragedy. "Emily, books have been written on the value of seeing a therapist after experiencing such a life-altering event. Once you have finally let go of your pain, it will be easier for you to take the next step forward. I'm not in the position to provide the help you need right now. I want you to feel better, but what I want and what you need are too different things. You'll learn the tools you need to move through your pain, but you have to be willing to share."

"But, Mom, I don't *like* to talk about it. Not with anyone. I'm afraid. I don't even know this person."

"All you need to know about her is that she's trained to work with those who have suffered the loss of loved ones. We aren't unique. She's heard stories similar to ours many other times. Trust her." Sitting outside the office, I watched as she shuffled through the doorway, peering at me one more time over her shoulder. I could see the dread in her eyes. "Please, God," I prayed silently, even as I wondered if He were listening to me, "help her express her feelings and put the right words in the mouth of this therapist. Ones that will help."

An hour later, as Emily walked towards me, I searched her eyes. They were red and swollen from crying. I breathed a sigh of relief. Finally, her bottled up emotions had broken through her wall of resistance. "How did it go?" I asked, wanting to pull her into my arms, but resisting. I was afraid I would break down again in public and she didn't need that.

"It was okay."

"I think you should return for at least one more session." She just looked at me and continued walking.

Emily did return several more times, but she never looked forward to the hour with the therapist and I knew she felt the same emptiness I had been feeling. Talking about the event and reading about other survivors of suicide wasn't enough. She needed something more. She needed God. So did I. Maybe I shouldn't give up. Maybe I shouldn't be so cynical. "Please God, comfort Emily's broken heart. Open your arms to her and bring her the peace she needs."

I prayed constantly for my children after that, hoping that a belief in God's healing power and growing a deeper and stronger faith was what we all needed. But knowing and believing something doesn't mean we will find instant consolation or understanding. The mind is a powerful organ and it operates in its own way and on its own time schedule. Depression, shock and denial continue to play havoc on our emotions, but as a mother, I had taken an important step in seeing to the mental health of my children.

Now, I needed to follow my own advice. I was certain that after my trip to Rockport and after falling apart at the group therapy session, I had no more tears to shed. I'd be able to discuss my greatest concerns and ask specific questions and receive answers that would bring peace of mind. I was mistaken. Being asked pointed questions about my feelings opened the dam again. But, like Christopher, I couldn't understand why constantly talking about the tragedy was helpful. Talking and talking and reliving the agony brought me no comfort. I *needed* comforting, before I could "move on."

Both children and I met with the therapist in one-on-one sessions twice a month for the rest of the summer. The expense became burdensome, because medical insurance didn't pay for the therapy. When school started again, we all stopped going. I also attended the support group meetings twice a month and checked out some of the material they had available for reading. Both experiences encouraged me to read as much about suicide survivors as I could. I made a trip to the bookstore and came home with whatever was on the shelf. Unfortunately, all the books were written by psychiatrists, psychologists, or counselors specializing in survivor therapy, sometimes in conjunction with a survivor. Some had experienced a suicide within their family. There was a similarity in the books, which focused on the stages of grief and the offering of very many very short stories of other suicide survivors, just like those I had heard in the support group. They talked about statistics and symptoms and reasons why people chose suicide.

None offered me any words of comfort. There was no comfort in hearing story after story of those who felt as isolated, ashamed, lonely, forgotten, and angry as I was.

But even so – and as painful as it was – every chapter of every book had something that made sense or that brought clarification. I wasn't any different from other suicide survivors. They had all gone through denial and abject shock and anger and shame and guilt and helplessness and depression. But no one talked about feeling *comforted* by all this information and the shared stories of grief that too often lingered for years or a lifetime. No one talked about how their faith in God had helped them through the dark days. No one talked about how their faith was the only thing that brought any real sense to the senseless act of suicide. No one talked about how they knew they'd see their once deeply troubled loved one again someday . . . in heaven.

That's when I realized God had not "taken" Bert from me. That was Bert's doing. God "permits" things to happen for a divine purpose we won't fully understand until much later . . . perhaps not before we stand in His presence. Bert had been gifted with the same free will God gave me and every other human being. We are free to choose how we will act or react to any given situation, even the trials and tribulations that come to every one of us. When we are unable to make wise choices, when our fear of the consequences of our past actions plague us to such an extent that we are unable to seek God's counsel or trust in His love and eagerness to provide the help we need, we may lapse into a depression that creates the inability to think rationally. We are unable to pull ourselves out of such a depression, without medical help. Doctors are God's servants, and they are given the wisdom to understand the workings of our minds. Ministers and priests are God's servants and are given the wisdom to understand the workings of our souls. We can learn a great deal about our minds and souls through reading and research and seeking counsel, but we will not fully have peace of mind until we can turn over our pain to God and leave our mental and soul healing in His hands.

Even before Bert ended his life, my routine had always been to wake up at five o'clock in the morning to read my Bible, pray, meditate, and write in my journal. I had gotten away from this practice during the first month of shock and denial . . . and anger. After reading the books on suicide, which promised to bring "healing and hope," and not experiencing a change in my all-day, every-day suffering, I returned to my Bible and to daily talks with my Heavenly Father.

> *God is our refuge and strength, an ever present help in trouble.* — Psalms 46:1 (NIV)

> *Peace I leave with you, my peace I give you. I do not give to you as the world gives. Do not let your heart be troubled and do not be afraid.* — John 14:27 (NIV)

This was the nourishment my soul yearned to hear. While I was in shock, denying that my husband would ever take his life and leave his family to suffer the consequences, and pointing the finger of blame at God for bringing such suffering upon all of us, I had forgotten that God brings "the peace that transcends all understanding." At the time of my most profound shock, my questions were the wrong ones. God had not abandoned me, even when my faith stumbled. He was there all along, waiting. Fortunately, He is patient and understanding. He understood why I resorted to ranting and raving at Him. He waited while I searched the Internet, while I read through a dozen books and articles on suicide, while I attended a support group and sought "professional" therapy. He didn't abandon me, even when I wished, like Job, that I had never been born so I wouldn't have to endure such profound pain. He knew I wasn't ready to come to Him for answers. My mind was in turmoil, my heart had hardened against Him, and I couldn't be quiet long enough to hear His voice.

Like Job who sought counsel from his friends, I had to seek the counsel of friends and of strangers in books and support groups. I had to listen to many voices, before I was ready to listen to His. God knew I needed to travel slowly in my blind journey toward truth and understanding and finally into His arms for the comforting I craved. Before I could stand tall and move one foot forward, before I could plead for courage and strength, I needed to be *comforted*. I needed reassurance that someone loved me unconditionally and forever and that life was worth living.

Finally, I was able to break through the barrier of my silence and begin to communicate with my children and other members of my family. Finally, I was able to communicate once again with God. But . . . I was still travelling blind and the emotional wreckage that came with Bert's suicide was not easily repaired. Grief still had a strangle hold on me and as I internalized my lingering pain, I feared I would lock it up in a prison of my own making.

. . . that through endurance and the encouragement of the Scriptures we might have hope. — Romans 15:4

Chapter 5

One Step Forward, Two Steps Back

By the end of my second month as a widow and suicide survivor, I still hadn't removed Bert's clothes from our closets or dresser drawers. It seemed too final. Several times, I opened his closet door with good intentions, but I'd stand there peering bleary-eyed at the assortment of shirts and sport coats, remembering how he looked in them on particular occasions. Then I'd close the door on both the clothes and the memories. I wanted — *needed* — everything to remain intact. The golfing shorts he had worn his last weekend at home were still on the stool in our closet, ready to be washed. I had not been able to pull open a single drawer holding his socks and underwear, and his shoes remained as he had left them, lined up in pairs: dress shoes, sneakers, boating shoes, and several pairs of cowboy boots, part of a Texan's wardrobe.

My brother-in-law had found a large-sized plastic trash bag filled with soiled jeans and shirts in the back seat of Bert's truck when he drove it back to San Antonio from Laredo. Normally, either Bert or I would take the clothes to the cleaners. In the turmoil of the first month, I hadn't known what to do with them. The bag remained in the trunk of my car. In the back of my mind, I knew the clothing would be given away eventually, but first, the items needed to be cleaned.

One morning, as I was drinking coffee with Sonya in the kitchen, I remembered the bag. "I have to do something with Bert's dirty ranch clothes today. They're still in the trunk of my car," I said. "I've put off taking them to the cleaners long enough."

Sonya placed her coffee cup carefully on the table. "Letty, for goodness sakes, why are you going to spend all that money at the cleaners? Why don't you just let me wash them?"

I shook my head. "It's kind of you to offer, Sonya, but you know that Bert likes the shirts heavily starched and his jeans pressed. It . . . it just wouldn't be the same."

Grabbing my hands and holding them tightly in hers, she peered directly into my eyes. "He's gone, Letty. He's not going to be wearing those things again. Not ever. It doesn't matter if they're pressed or starched. They just need to be clean before you give them away. How about if you let me wash them, and then if you still think you want to take them to the cleaners later, you can do that."

I was hesitant at first, but finally agreed. It was a small decision, but I made it. Sonya would wash the clothes. Then I'd decide if they should hang in Bert's closet or go to charity. It was another step forward.

Chris had not changed his mind and planned to transfer to Southwest Texas State University in San Marcos to continue his education. It wasn't far from San Antonio, only an hour's drive, but I knew I would miss having him in the house for purely selfish reasons. The last thing I wanted was for him to feel guilty about leaving, though. He needed to live his own life and make plans for his future. I wanted him to feel the excitement and joy that comes with fulfilling each goal, however inconsequential, and that first goal was to leave home for the college experience and growth of independence. While concerned with fitting in and being accepted, he would learn that every choice, every decision he made would result in either a positive return or a negative consequence. Both would contribute to molding his character.

Every mother worries that her children will make the wrong choices, get in with the wrong crowd, tarnish their reputations and bring a shame they will live with for the rest of their lives. While they are under our care, we can watch over them, but once they're on their own, we can only pray. I remembered hearing President Nixon say in one of his speeches that if we take no risks, we'll suffer no defeats, but if we don't take risks, we won't win any victories either. I wanted Chris to have many victories. His first would be to survive Bert's suicide, to learn from it, and

51

to determine what he needed to do to make wiser choices in his own life. I couldn't ignore the fact that he'd be hesitant to bring his new friends home for visits. I wanted him to be confident that I wouldn't "rain on his parade." That meant I had to project more positivity about my own future. It was hard. Very hard.

Although it was only the middle of July, Emily was already looking forward to starting high school as a freshman cheerleader. She had spent a year in a class of the oldest students in the middle school; now she would be in a class of the youngest in her new school. The beginning weeks would be challenging, as she, too, made new friends and dealt with the transitions that come with teenage angst. She would need my support and encouragement. I didn't want her to grow up too fast, and it was critical for me to establish rules we could both respect and adhere to without reservation. It would be a difficult year for both of us, as our mother-daughter dynamic changed. I would miss Bert's wise counsel and knew I had to step up and be willing to keep the doors of communication open. Right now, that was still a struggle for me. Merely thinking about what the future months would bring seemed like a burden I couldn't bear. I wanted to flick a switch on the wall and have every problem and perceived problem go away as quickly as the light in a room does when its energy source is removed.

I thought often about my stepson, Bert Michael. Although he lived far away, I wanted to maintain contact with him; it's what Bert would want me to do. I didn't know how to go about this. How should I approach him? Did he care? Was he even interested in keeping up our relationship? How was he dealing with his personal anguish? My mind would go into overdrive worrying about him. I spoke with his grandparents as often as I could to get reports, but they didn't know much. They didn't like to intrude and rarely asked questions beyond, "How are you doing?" My feelings of helplessness seemed to be growing, and I wanted to scream in frustration and disappointment, but I kept my thoughts to myself.

I worried, worried, worried about everything. The cars, the yard and upkeep of our home, our ranch in Laredo, our finances, but most of all the children. Bert was the one who had disciplined them when it was needed.

I was too soft. He was firm, but in a loving way. Tough love. He wanted nothing but the best for them and didn't shy away from discussing the problems that arose. He set and enforced our rules concerning everything from staying out too late, to not finishing homework on time, to the overuse of all the technology games and gadgets that are a part of our lives, including cellphone use. How was I going to handle all these issues by myself? It's not that Chris and Emily didn't have their birth father close by. They did and he loved them, too, but it wasn't the same. They lived with us, and Bert had helped me raise them on a daily basis. He had been actively involved with their school work, sports, teachers, and friends. He was always on top of things. I could go to him with every concern, regardless of how insignificant it was. Now, he would no longer be available to me as my sounding board.

Not a single day went by without the shedding of tears. Despite my good intentions when I returned from my short stay at the coast, I still voiced my fervent wish that Bert would just "come home." Regardless of what I had heard or learned in the support group and from my therapist, I seemed to have no control over my thoughts or vacillating emotions. The analogy is often made that a tragedy of mammoth proportion puts us in the front seat of a roller coaster. It speeds up and down and whips around corners as we scream hysterically in our fear, wishing all the while we could get off to plant our feet on solid ground again. I seemed to be in overdrive on one of those roller coasters from dawn to dusk and would become irrationally angry at little things (like my father wanting to eat dinner an hour after he had already had his dinner), or miserably morose, because all the joy had been sucked out of my life, or completely overwhelmed and impatient with the nonstop pressure of having to make decisions.

I did have moments when I could climb out of my personal prison and tackle a project. For short intervals, I could finally focus my thoughts on the task at hand. The second I finished it, however, another wave of sorrow would suck me in and I would feel as if I were drowning. I kept count of the days since that fateful Wednesday morning and knew almost to the hour how long I had survived without hearing Bert's voice. Each additional day seemed like a mini-miracle.

During this second month, I became increasingly weighed down by all the paperwork that needed my attention. Insurance documents, removing Bert's name from credit cards, writing my own will, dealing with the funeral expenses, Chris' college financial aid papers, and Emily's high school documents, including permission slips and cheerleading forms . . . everything needed reading for understanding and then signing. Medical records showed immunizations needed updating. Everything had a deadline, which added to my stress. The piles on my desk didn't seem to diminish. I'd sign checks with tears streaming down my cheeks, always conscious of the eyes of my parents on me. Although they didn't question why I was so upset every day, I worried about their thoughts regarding the changes in our household and how it was affecting their health.

The day arrived when I had to make my first visit to the cemetery for both business and a visit to the gravesite. Emily and I went with my sister-in-law to pour over the options available for the design of Bert's headstone. "I can't believe I'm doing this," I whispered, blinking away the quick rush of tears that blinded me from seeing anything clearly.

"I'm so sorry, Letty," Pearl said, "but this is something you need to do. A year from now, you'd regret not having personal input. I wouldn't feel right about making choices for you."

Colored brochures showing samples of headstones were spread out on the table for our perusal. After taking a quick look at several, I covered my face with shaking hands and cried. Once again, I was faced with a reality I wasn't ready to accept. As my sobs dwindled, the silence in the room became deafening. I finally glanced at Emily and saw the mixture of concern and impatience in her eyes. I hated that she perceived of me as being weak and incapable of dealing with death and stress. Women are supposed to be the backbone of the family. Strong, courageous, independent, capable. The nurturer. I was failing in every category

Once I regained my composure, the saleswoman went through her routine. "I'm assuming that since you selected a double plot, you're planning to be buried with your husband. Would you like to have your name engraved on the headstone also? This is often done by the surviving spouse."

I didn't hesitate. "Yes, of course."

Emily was shocked. "Wait a minute, Mom. Don't I have a say about this? I don't like the idea of seeing your name on a gravestone. Please don't put it on there. It's going to be years and years before it needs to be done."

I looked helplessly at the saleswoman for an appropriate answer. There was no question in my mind about the procedure, but I could understand Emily's concern.

"It's very common for people who know they're going to be buried with their spouse some day to inscribe their names on the headstone when one of them passes away. That way, the carving is performed by the same person and at a lesser cost."

"But . . . what if you marry again, Mom? And even if you don't, the headstone has to be taken up anyway to insert the date of your . . . you know . . . ." She pushed a few of the brochures into a pile, unable to speak the unspeakable. "What's the difference if your name is engraved then or now? None of that reasoning makes sense. Those rules are for old people, not for one's your age."

"I'm not going to remarry," I said firmly. Right then, even the thought of such a thing seemed implausible. Bert was the love of my life. No one could take his place.

When we finished the transaction, we headed for the gravesite. As we drove slowly on the winding road through the cemetery, I peered out the window at the dozens of headstones representing the lives of others who had left this world. From the appearance of the markers and the grass and other plantings around them, many had obviously died years ago. I wondered if any had died at their own hand, like Bert.

When we reached the site of Bert's grave, Pearl parked the car and we walked across the grass to a stone bench nearby. We sat in silence and stared at the still freshly groomed plot, each with our own thoughts. Then, almost on cue, we began to cry. Choking back my sobs, I wailed again, "Why did you leave me like that, Bert? Why did you do this to us? We . . . we're suffering. We miss you. We . . . we *need* you." As we huddled together, I wondered if it had been a mistake to come. It was taking two steps back in our recovery. Memories of the shocking news were still too fresh, too easily revived, too painful to relive.

Although it wasn't unexpected, another event occurred that took a toll on our already fragile emotional states. About four months before Bert's suicide, our beloved Labrador, Trout, became so ill we had to put him in a veterinary hospital for a few days. The vet diagnosed the problem as pancreatitis. His hospital stay, including x-rays, other tests and medications quickly added up to a couple of thousand dollars. "What are we going to do?" I asked Bert. "We've spent so much money, and Trout doesn't seem to be getting better."

"He's part of the family, honey. We can't let him die without doing whatever is humanly possible to save him. He's worth more than money to us."

When Trout returned home from the hospital, he came down with a severe case of kennel cough, which lasted for a good five or six weeks. During that time, we made frequent visits to the vet as he continued to lose his appetite and retain fluids. After Bert's funeral, it seemed that Trout's condition declined rapidly. We could tell he was miserable and forlorn. He seemed to know Bert wasn't around any more and he missed him. Although Chris and Emily had begged to get a dog, it was really Bert who wanted one the most. He said he'd get one only on the condition we named him Trout. Since Bert was an avid fisherman, we unanimously agreed to accept that silly name for a dog.

Over time, we came to like the name and admitted no other name would've suited him. Trout was greatly loved, and he gave us as much joy as we gave him a good life. While we were dealing with our grief over Bert's absence from our family unit, we watched with concern as Trout seemed to grow weaker. It was as though he didn't have the strength or desire to go on living without his master.

One morning, I rose early from bed to get ready for another trip to the doctor with my dad, who was suffering physically from several medical problems. In the two years he and mother had been living with us, he had endured several surgeries for circulation issues due to his COPD and congestive heart failure stemming from a high cholesterol problem. Increasingly, he had also been affected by a form of dementia, typical in as many as one in two of our elderly. My father was in his eighties. Without Sonya's help, I would not have been able to take care of him . . . especially now.

After dressing for the doctor's appointment, I went to the kitchen to let Trout out of the house. He was unable to stand up. Hugging him and with tears rolling down my cheeks, I thought immediately of Bert. How would the children, how would I be able to endure the loss of another family member? Again, I went to Christopher's room as the heralder of bad news. "Wake up, son, it's Trout. He's very ill. I think you'll have to take him to the vet, while I take your grandfather to see his doctor." Hugging him, I softly whispered, "He can't stand up, Chris, and he's whimpering."

Without hesitation, Chris leaped from his bed, pulled on his jeans and a shirt and dashed to the kitchen where Trout was lying. He gently picked him up, carried him to his truck, and headed straight to the vet.

While at the doctor's office, I received a call from the vet. "How is he?" I asked, knowing the answer without having to hear his report.

"He's pretty sick, Letty. There's really nothing else we can do for him."

"If this were your beloved family pet, what would you do? I-I'm not able to make a decision right now."

"I'd put him down, Letty. He's suffering and there's no sense in prolonging his misery."

I fought to control my trembling bottom lip and sighed inwardly. How could my already broken heart ever mend? "All r-right," I said, my voice breaking. "Do what you have to do. Put him down."

"I'm really sorry, Letty. I know this is a difficult time for you and your children. It's a painless process and quick, if that's any comfort to you."

As I hung up the phone, I ached for Chris who would have to witness Trout's death as he slipped out of this life and into the next one. I was thankful his girlfriend was with him for support. He wouldn't have to drive home alone. When I retuned later, I found the two of them lying quietly on the living room floor staring blankly up at the ceiling. I found a place next to Christopher and reached for his hand. "How are you doing, son? I know this was an especially difficult experience for you right now. Thank you for taking care of Trout. Were you with him when he died?"

He nodded. "It was horrible, Mom. Really sad. It's not like he suffered. It's just that . . . well, it seemed like he knew what was happening. He turned his head away from me, like he couldn't stand to see me hurting by what was about to happen. It was hard to let him go, but he died very peacefully. Like he had fallen asleep. At least he's not suffering anymore."

Trout wasn't suffering. Bert wasn't suffering. But Chris, Emily, and I were. Bereft once again, I questioned God's wisdom. "Why now?" I cried to Him. "Why couldn't you have waited a while longer? We have enough on our plate. You promised you wouldn't give us more than we could bear! We've had enough!"

A week or so later, Emily and I were having lunch together. "What would you say to our making a trip to Dallas to visit Aunt Elva and Uncle Dick?" I asked her. "We could fly and, if you'd like, you could take a friend with us."

She was quiet for some time and then, somewhat hesitantly, said,"I guess so, Mom."

"I think it would be good for both of us, honey. Get us out of the house. It's not really a summer vacation, but I promise we'll do some fun things while there. The distraction will get our minds off all the sorrow we're feeling and we won't be surrounded with so many reminders of Bert and Trout." Although I was still taking something to help me sleep, Emily had been struggling with insomnia and nightmares for weeks. I was hoping a change of scenery would help her get the sleep and rest she so desperately needed.

In my quiet moments, I would catch myself thinking about death and dying. I wondered if people knew they were dead, and if they could really "see" their loved ones go about their daily lives. I wondered if they ever wanted to return to this world, and if they recognized family members and friends who had passed away before them. I wondered if people in heaven looked the same as the day they died and whether or not they could influence the behavior of those they had left behind. Especially, I wondered if Bert knew Trout had died. And were there pet dogs in heaven . . . or only human beings who believed in Jesus as God's son and our Savior.

My brother-in-law Dick picked us up at the Dallas airport. We were quiet on the car trip, spending the time peering vacantly out the window, alone with our thoughts. As we entered my sister's house, she and her grandchildren welcomed us with open arms. "We've planned some surprises for you," one of them said, grinning shyly. All of them were visibly excited about giving us their homemade welcome gifts and notes.

The children had wrapped their gifts themselves with copious amounts of masking tape. They knew Bert had died, but they were too young to understand the grieving state of mind. Seven-year olds do understand sadness, however, and they went out of their way to make us feel happy. In unison, they said, "Aunt Letty, in the morning we're going to have a surprise for you and Emily, and her friend Grace, too. All of you." Their grins were infectious, and I felt my spirits rise.

We awoke in the morning to the sounds of chatter and whispering. My sister entered our bedroom with three hats and three floral neck scarves in different styles and colors. "As part of your surprise, you must choose which hat and scarf to wear. When you're ready, come into the playroom where your surprise will be waiting."

"We're still in our pajamas. Do we get dressed first?"

"The girls don't care what clothing you're wearing, as long as you don the required hat and scarf. Don't take too long."

Five minutes later, we entered the playroom to see a typical little girls' tea party, with the child's size table set with dishes and even name tags to mark where we should be seated. They had thought of every detail, including the playing of soft music to provide atmosphere. The menu consisted of hot chocolate in tiny tea cups, cookies, orange slices, and mints placed in the center of the table. We spent the next several minutes sitting around the table chatting about the silly things little girls enjoy.

Then one of the girls brought out a deck of Old Maid cards. The famous card game never fails to bring smiles and groans as the old maid card is chosen from those fanned out in chubby hands. Emily and I looked at each other and smiled . . . perhaps for the first time in two months.

Most of the time, my sister's presence and talkativeness pushed back the thoughts of Bert that had dominated my mind for so many weeks. With a pool in the backyard, we spent a great deal of time in the sun, watching the younger ones play in the water. We ate delicious food and watched DVD movies in the evenings. During any lull in activity, an overwhelming sadness would take hold of me, and I would struggle to hold back the tears. This wasn't the time or place for them. It was important to give Emily a complete reprieve from moroseness.

During our visit, I spoke with my sister about the increasing care needed by our parents. "Elva, I need your help. I've had Mom and Dad in our home for the past couple of years, and with Sonya's caregiving every day, it has worked out fine. Now, with . . . with Bert gone, I-I'm just not able to deal with the daily problems that arise." I impatiently brushed a few tears from my cheeks. "I need a break, Elva. Would it be possible for you to take them for a couple of weeks?"

"Of course. Don't you worry about it. Dick and I will drive you home and bring them back with us. They can stay here until we have the opportunity to talk about a more permanent arrangement. Maybe it's time we think about a retirement home or assisted living facility."

Neither Emily nor I were ready to pack up and head for home. We knew we'd feel the silence of Bert's absence as soon as we entered the house. And we did, but we had both taken another step forward by allowing ourselves to relax and have moments of enjoyment again. That was a good thing.

Each day, I was making small decisions, usually of no major consequences. Although my brother had assisted with the major ones that came shortly after the funeral, I knew it was time for me to think hard about the future and what was best for all of us. I was facing another dilemma, one that most women usually pass on to their husbands. I was still driving my six-year old Mercedes, but it had needed several repairs during this time and I was concerned about what I'd do if the car broke down. With Bert gone and Chris going away to college, I wouldn't have their assistance. I didn't want to add the hassle and expense of maintaining the aging car to my already full worry list. And I worried about keeping up with the payments.

After much thought and discussion with Chris and my brother, I decided to notify the bank. The car was listed only in Bert's name. They agreed to take back the car and sell it to pay off what was left of the loan.

When some life insurance money came in, I made the decision to purchase a less expensive but more reliable vehicle, a Volkswagon Passat. As I sat at the Volkswagen dealership, I held another silent pity party, wishing I didn't have to be there. I wished Bert were alive. I wished Chris had already finished college and would be living at home until he married. I wished my dad were still his old self and able to help me. Then I kicked myself with a reminder that one of my roles as a mother was to teach my daughter the importance of being independent, of knowing how to deal with issues like buying and trading cars, and of having the confidence and know-how to conduct a business transaction. It all sounded so easy. It wasn't. I was terrified. What if I were being handed jargon and ended up overpaying for the Passat? The young saleswoman who wrote up the transaction must have noticed my look of despondency. I certainly wasn't exuding any sense of enthusiasm.

"Mrs. Lozano, why aren't you happy? You're buying a brand new Volkswagen Passat at a very good price."

I looked at her and forced the semblance of a smile. There was no reason to share with her the reason for my placidity. I signed the papers and drove home in my new vehicle. The successful transaction represented one more major decision. Another step forward.

Every evening, I'd cross the day off my mental calendar. I had survived another twenty-four hours as a widow. If time heals, like all the books and therapists say, it meant I was closer to some sort of closure on my grieving process. Although those in my position said it took months and even years to fully recover, I was making a greater effort to be the mother and daughter and sister and friend I used to be. I was seeking therapy, reading about being a suicide survivor, reading my Bible, and praying. I was doing all the legwork, and in my fragile state of mind, I finally accepted that God had never abandoned me. I had abandoned Him. He was there with open arms waiting for me to come to Him with all my sorrows and uncertainties. If I truly believed He would use this horrendous experience to guide me toward my future destiny, I needed to stay close to Him, seek His guidance, and listen carefully for his voice.

Jon Walker, editor of the *Daily Hope Devotionals* and author of *Costly Grace*, wrote a devotional for the emailed daily series of Rick Warren's *Daily Hope* (author of *The Purpose Driven Life* and pastor of Saddleback Church in California). It said what I knew in my heart, but had pushed aside during my weeks of denial and shock, but now the verse from the first letter to the Corinthians brought comfort to me.

> When we make choices disconnected and independent from God, there is little difference between the way we live our lives and the way non-believers live their lives. *'But people who aren't Christians can't understand these truths from God's Spirit. It all sounds foolish to them because only those who have the Spirit can understand what the Spirit means.'* (1 Corinthians 2:14 NLT) You have the Holy Spirit inside you. You have the ability to understand when God is telling you to take steps toward his goals for your life. Ask him to teach you to hear his still small voice and to help you take the steps he tells you to take. Then, look for the ways he guides you through the decisions and details of your life." (March 24, 2011, *Daily Hope* with Rick Warren)

It meant a great deal to me, during these initial weeks of grieving, to have the full support of Bert's family. They made me feel welcome with their continuous caring, words of comfort, and offers of assistance. In any time of great stress and tragedy, family and friends are important links between reality and our self-imposed mental imprisonment. This is especially true when we blame ourselves for the suicide, thinking we must have done something to set off the reaction. We worry that others will blame us, too. I thought that under the circumstances of ours being a second marriage and with no "blood" grandchildren to bind us, Bert's family would soon exclude me from their circle. Fortunately, that hadn't happened. Bert was the link that brought us together; now he would continue to be the link that keeps us together. We need each other. As more time passes, I more fully understand the importance of this continuing connection.

On June 21st, Father's Day, we felt the loss of Bert's presence even more than on other days. Families are like a puzzle. When there is a missing piece, the picture is not complete. Normally, the children and I would plan something special for the day. A meal of favorite foods, gifts, and lots of praise. Three generations in the same house, celebrating all the men who have become role models and the caretakers of our family and family traditions. Not just Bert and my father, but the children's birth father and all the uncles and brothers who influenced our lives, teaching us many of the skills we need for self-reliance. Bert was the glue that held our family together. He was the embodiment of trust and genuine compassion, worthy of admiration and respect. That's why his final act was so difficult to understand and accept.

During these first couple of months, I avoided my customary full-cart grocery store excursions. Instead, I would make small trips and buy only the absolute necessities. I stopped watching television shows. Those depicting couples were too difficult to watch, and those featuring murders and the tragic loss of life brought nothing but stress. I no longer had a need to go to the dry cleaners on a weekly basis. I couldn't face even the contemplation of driving to our ranch and wasn't sure when I would ever be strong enough to do so. I didn't look forward to the weekends; in fact, I came to dread them. They usually consisted of staying in my pajamas and trying to sleep as much as I could in order to lessen the time spent in reliving the once joyful time when Bert would return from the ranch and we could be together.

The only thing I could do with any regularity was write in my journal, especially in the early morning hours. It gave me the opportunity to release my pent-up emotions. The numbness that followed the news of Bert's death was starting to wear off and replacing it was the full impact of what had happened. I was close to becoming totally dysfunctional. It was the diligence of my family members that kept me going. That, and knowing God was watching and waiting and loving me, and believing that He had a purpose for my life.

Although I had taken a few hesitant steps forward in facing the rest of my life, I was still taking two steps backward whenever I was forced to face the reality of what I had once thought a normal world. The road back to sanity for a suicide survivor is a slow and painful journey, fraught with seemingly endless setbacks. Those who leave God out of the equation find it even more difficult to understand why life is worth living. My daily prayer was for Him to speak loudly through the Holy Spirit living within me and to give me the patience and ability to hear His voice. He is called the great physician, because He heals our wounded spirits and broken dreams.

The Lord is a stronghold for the oppressed, a stronghold in times of trouble . . . he does not forget the cry of the afflicted. —Psalm 9:9, 12 (NIV)

My God shall supply all of your needs. —Philippians 4:19 (NASB)

Chapter 6

Memories and Mayhem

While my parents were in Dallas with my sister Elva, I wrestled continuously with my guilt over sending them away from what had been their home for two years and the longing to be alone to process where I had been and where I was headed. It had been years since I'd put myself first for anything. All too soon, my parents would want to return, but I knew I wasn't nearly ready to take on the full responsibility for their increasing needs. It was enough for me to take care of myself and the children.

As the days progressed into August, the sundry tasks of getting Chris and Emily prepared for another school year occupied much of my time. I tried to focus on the buying of school supplies and necessary fall clothing, and then helping Chris pack up a long list of "stuff" for his college venture. For short periods of time, my mind was diverted from thinking of other things, although I found myself becoming increasingly anxious and restless, and my thoughts would leap from one subject to another. I daydreamed continuously and found it difficult to follow the kid's conversations. Even into the third month since Bert's death, I was far from being myself.

During this same period, I reached out to Bert's son in Mexico and extended an invitation for him and his family to come to San Antonio for a visit. My heart was saddened when his mother relayed his message: Bert Michael saw no reason to make such summer trips anymore, now that his father was dead. My heart ached for him, but I understood. Our connection through Bert would always exist, but it wouldn't have the same bond. My children had looked forward to seeing him, since he was such a strong part of the man who had fathered them throughout their entire childhoods. I had thought spending time together would bring the three of them some much needed comfort, but explained to Christopher and Emily that we shouldn't take Bert Michael's decision personally. We were not in a position to judge how he should grieve for his father. Perhaps it was still too painful for him to be in our company. Too many reminders, too many memories of happier times. I relayed the message to his mother that our invitation would remain open, and they were both welcome in our home whenever he changed his mind.

Often, when Bert Michael made his summer pilgrimage from Mexico to our home, he would bring his younger half-brother, Diego, with him. We had become close to him, too. The summer before Bert's death, we had all enjoyed a trip to Acapulco. Bert had taken Diego aside to let him know he would always be part of our family, because of his relationship to Bert Michael. If there was anything he ever needed, all he had to do was ask, as he was like a son to him and was loved by all of us. Now, circumstances had changed everything. If we adults cannot endure the shock and sorrow that comes with the news of a suicide, how much more painful it must be for children who live so far away, but love with the same full hearts. The two boys have become part of my daily prayers. God will embrace and watch over them in Bert's absence. The memories of our many joyful times together will remain with me always and, hopefully, with them too. I look forward to the time when we can all be together and share them without the shedding of tears.

With Chris and Emily back in school and out of the house during the daytime and my parents in Dallas, I was totally alone for hours, another new experience for me and one I welcomed. For years, there had been a steady parade of other people coming and going. Before Bert came into my life, I had never liked being alone. Fear of the unknown haunted me. Now I had the freedom to wander throughout the entire house, relish the memories, and talk to Bert. I could express my feelings and feel deeply about whatever was in my heart without being conscious of watchful eyes.

Surprisingly, my hope of Bert's returning to our home hadn't faded, despite my good intentions, and I recognized how powerful denial is when we have suffered such a mind-blowing shock. Although I had read about denial in the books I'd purchased and heard other survivors speak of their own hopes at the few group meetings I'd attended, I had readily dismissed the accounts. Then, while I was in my initial state of shock, they were only words and held no meaning for me. Now? To be honest, a part of me wanted to stay stuck, because hope delayed my having to think too far into a future with nameless uncertainties. Why make plans when they can be shattered in an instant with one phone call? I was rational enough to know that once I accepted the truth with any degree of finality, there'd be no turning back. That thought scared me.

I spent considerable time reading my Bible, in addition to secular materials about what to do when tragedy enters our life, and then I poured all my thoughts and feelings into journal entries. Writing seemed to help. It was as though I were having a conversation with Bert or myself. But again, words were just that. Words. Over and over again, I'd ask myself why I couldn't simply believe that *"All things work together for good to them that love God. . . ."* Roman 8:28, (KJV) If my belief and faith were strong enough, I should know that since God had not put the gun in Bert's hands and ordered him to pull the trigger, He was actively working to ensure something positive would come of the Lozano family tragedy. He was weeping with me and for me, and my knowing that should be putting my fears and feelings of helplessness to rest.

Despite our faith, we fall back into old habits. We want to do things for ourselves. We become impatient and want immediate answers and clear solutions. When they don't come and the days and weeks pass and we still feel miserable, our faith falters and we begin listening to the voices of doubting Thomases. Obviously, my faith was weak, and it needed strengthening if I ever expected to move on. Time and again, I reminded myself, *I can do all things, through Christ who strengthens me.*

As August drew to a close I knew I wasn't ready for my parents to come home. Picking up on what Elva had mentioned, I finally gave in to my qualms and phoned my sister Laura. With a lump lodged firmly in my throat and tears hovering on the rims of my eyelids, I waited to hear her voice. "Laura? I'm so sorry to bother you. I . . . I'm struggling to come up with the right words. I'm just not ready for Mother and Daddy to come home. I still need to be alone. Is there any way you could take them for a while? I don't want them to see how much I'm still hurting, and I don't want to feel like I have to bottle up my feelings. I'm afraid I'll come to resent their being here, when I'm having another bad day and have to tend to their needs. I don't want to cause problems for any of you. I feel so guilty, but —"

"Hey, slow down! You don't have to feel guilty about anything, Letty. I fully understand. We all do. Don't worry about it. And you certainly don't have to apologize for anything either. We'll make other arrangements. You've been a godsend these past couple of years having them in your home. We've been talking about it. We thought we should look into something more permanent . . . a retirement home facility. If you'd like, you can come with us to choose the one that best suits their needs."

After our conversation, I felt relieved. Even though Sonya had been with us most of the two years, I was the one who had to intervene whenever my mom or dad dissolved into one of their moods. Mom, who'd had a stroke when she was only sixty-one, had only limited use of her right side and had lost the clarity of her speech. Her mind, however, was perfectly intact twenty-some years later, and she would show her irritation when Dad napped too much by waking him up, causing another argument. Dad, who had cared for her in their home for years, had finally developed a series of medical problems of his own, including the slow descent into dementia. He often refused to take his medications, didn't want to shower, or didn't feel like eating. In the torrid heat of the Texas summer day, he'd don his jacket and cowboy hat and sit outside for hours just staring at his old Hummer in our driveway. At times, he'd forget he was no longer able to drive, and we'd have to hide the car keys. Eventually, my sister Lisa bought it for her daughter to use, which helped Dad financially and kept us from having to sell it to a complete stranger.

Some days, Dad was fine with this sale, but on others, he'd become furious and decide we were conniving to get rid of his things in order to steal his money. To appease him and put this issue to rest, I told him that Bert and I had decided to give him our Tahoe as a gift. He was happy for a while, until he would see it missing from the driveway on weekends when Bert was home. Then we'd have to create other stories. "Bert took the Tahoe to have the oil changed, Dad." Or, "Bert noticed that a couple of the tires needed air." Or, "Bert took it into the shop for a tune-up today."

More difficult for me were the times when Dad would wake up at all hours of the night and want to go outside. He'd pull on some clothes and say, "I have to go somewhere, Letty. I don't want to be late." Then he'd admit, "I just don't remember where I'm supposed to be." It became necessary for us to follow him about as you would a toddler, for fear he'd fall and hurt himself or wander off someplace and get lost. He was a handful, even for Sonya and Jessica, another caregiver who would come to spend the night. Both parents needed my help. Help I wasn't ready or able to provide yet.

A couple of days after talking with Laura, we set a date for all of us siblings in San Antonio to check out retirement homes. Once we had decided on the right facility for their needs, we packed up their things from my house and hauled them to their new home. After decorating the few rooms, we had everything ready by the time Elva drove them back to San Antonio. Unfortunately, our choice only worked for a couple of months. My parents didn't like it, and we were all unhappy with the limited care they received. We realized, too late, the facility was really more of a retirement community for those who could live entirely on their own. Our parents both needed an assisted living environment, one that provided close supervision and help with everyday tasks and meals. So once again we searched for something more suitable and eventually found a place closer to our homes that everyone liked and would put our growing concerns to rest.

Some of the mayhem that had defined my life since mid-May settled down and I worked at establishing a workable routine that would get me through the long days filled with a mixture of both pleasant and unbearably dreadful memories.

I felt that as Bert's widow, he would not only want me to keep in contact with his son, but he'd want me to remain in close contact with his parents and other members of his family. He had called them on a regular basis and played golf with his dad, his brother-in-law Jay, and my brother Pete almost every Sunday. Now his father stepped in to be strong for me in my weakness. I remember one phone call when his words were particularly comforting. "Letty," he said, "you need to do whatever you're used to doing; whether it's going to get your hair cut or colored, or your nails manicured, or whatever else was in your old routine. Don't stop doing the things you enjoyed. Don't give up living, just because Bert isn't here to see you. Your kids are. And other people are looking to see how you handle yourself. Be an example for them."

The reason I remember this conversation so well is because only a few days before I had looked in the mirror and thought, "I look old and haggard and I feel as old as I look." I didn't care. The roots of my hair showed how gray I had become, and under normal circumstances, I would have rushed off to the hair salon. Keeping my hair colored and styled and my nails manicured made Bert happy. He was proud of me and liked to show me off. "Honey, you're such a girl," he'd say. Although I certainly enjoyed personal pampering, I had groomed myself mostly for him. Since he was no longer around to see me, I had developed the attitude, "Who cares? Why bother?" When my father-in-law told me to keep up my appearance, it was as though the message had come directly from Bert. I made the call to my salon to resume my standing appointments. Sometimes, when we look in the mirror and see the vision of what we used to be, a spark of energy returns and the day takes on a new color. Yes, appearances are deceiving, as they don't reveal what is happening to our hearts and souls; but the appearance of confidence that a little makeup or well-groomed hair or a fresh shirt provides is often enough to buck up our spirits.

One night Chris was home for the weekend, and I awakened to a sound and saw him staring down at me. His eyes were swollen and red. I glanced at the clock next to my bed. It was three o'clock in the morning. "What's the matter, son? Has something happened?" I sat up in alarm.

"I'm having a really bad night," he said, and tears rolled down his cheeks as he pressed his hands against his heart. "It hurts. My heart just . . . h-hurts." I reached out to pull him close and my own tears mingled with his. "I-I've been sitting outside in Bert's truck for about two hours just listening to all the songs that remind me of him. Will you come outside and sit with me? I want you to hear some of them."

I followed him to the truck and sat with him until dawn while we listened to the music that Bert had enjoyed while on the road between San Antonio and Laredo. I reached for Chris's hand. "It seems like it'll never get easier for us, doesn't it? I understand why this experience has touched you so deeply, Chris. Music of any kind has the ability to bring up all kinds of emotional responses. When you combine the lyrics, tempo, and rhythm of this particular music with your memories of Bert, it makes you feel sad today. A month from now, the same music may arouse a happier response. Years from now, hearing these songs will cause you to remember this night, but also the happier times when you probably sang along with Bert while hearing it."

"I guess you're right, Mom." He heaved a great sigh and peered out the windshield of the truck. "It's not just the music though. I go through all kinds of different feelings in just one day. I go from being mad at Bert, to feeling guilty about being mad. Then I get sad, because he thought he didn't have another way out of his own pain. It hurts so much, because I loved him and wished I'd known what was bothering him. Sometimes, I wonder what my life would be like if it hadn't been for him. I know he changed your life and that he loved us all more than anything, but I feel cheated that I never had the chance to really thank him and let him know how much I admired and respected him. I-I want to be like him, Mom, but I don't think I could ever fill his shoes. He was just too big . . . too big of a man. You know?"

Memories. They're wonderful and wearing at the same time. They come and go, flitting through our minds like birds in flight, leaving us either euphoric or emotionally drained. As a parent who has always tried to soothe and comfort members of the family who are hurting, there is no greater feeling of inadequacy or helplessness as when you're in the same miserable condition and unable to do or say anything to ease the situation. So we listen and nod and cry.

"You'll be all he was and more, son. Believe it. Act on it. Go ahead and remember Bert, but fill your own shoes. My heart is aching, too. Right now, we have to allow ourselves all the time we need to grieve. Unfortunately, it's not a quick process. Things will get better . . . in time."

"It comes out of nowhere, Mom. My heartache. I can't even predict when it's going to happen. I want to just run, but it's like . . . where do I go? I feel trapped inside my own body."

"Didn't the counseling sessions help you?"

"A little, but I got tired of rehashing the same stuff. I'm tired of feeling this way, too. It's hard to concentrate on my studies and sometimes I don't want to be with anyone at school. I still feel like . . . different. Like everybody's looking at me. Talking about me. Blaming me."

"All those kids . . . they're mainly focused on themselves, Chris. Not on you. College is tough. Everyone wants to be liked and looked up to. They might glance at you, but they're not really seeing you. They're thinking about themselves. If you see someone whose eyes are on you, nod or give them a finger-wiggle wave in response."

My response sounded so lame and inadequate. Like I felt at that moment. "Just always remember you are loved by everyone in our family, son. I'm glad you came to me and didn't keep how you're feeling to yourself. Do you remember what Bert used to say? *'It is what it is.'* We can't change what has already happened. We can't be the person we were before it happened. All we can do is to pray and ask for God's blessing and comfort and guidance . . . about everything. That's what I'm trying to do. I don't think Bert was in his right mind at the time, but I believe God is going to use this tragedy to help me become a better mother for you and your sister, and for you kids to become more independent and strong as you learn how really tough life is. God will help us all through this mountainous trial and give us the courage to prepare ourselves for the coming challenges. You must believe that, son. I do know this, too. Bert would be proud of you — the way you're handling this and how you've stepped up to help your sister and me. I'm grateful to you for that."

As I peered through the dim light of dawn at my son, I realized he was a reflection of Bert. He had some of his mannerisms, and he had already acquired many of his values and beliefs. That realization brought me a glimmer of joy. The first such feeling in a long, long time.

During this month of busyness and introspection and continued grief, I came to remember that in other times of difficulty — for instance the unexpected and wounding divorce from my first husband — God had provided immeasurable comfort and blessings in abundance. This remembrance brought back a verse that had spoken to me of God's promise. *"Truly I say to you, you will weep and lament . . . you will be sorrowful, but your sorrow will turn into joy."* John 16:19-20, (RSV) My sorrow had, indeed, turned into unspeakable joy when God brought Bert into my life to love me and to help me raise my two special children. As I contemplated that truth, I prayed for God's blessings once again, that my new journey from great grief and sagging faith would bring restored hope . . . hope that I could share with my still suffering children and family members and, perhaps, to others who were struggling with their own heartache as a suicide survivor.

God is a great and good God. He was patient with my failure to act on what I claimed to believe and very understanding of my inability to feel or show gratitude and appreciation for the little things that brought physical comfort to my daily life while I waited for the healing of my mental anguish. Although I had been handed an unexpected and mind-numbing trial, I still had my air-conditioned home, reliable transportation, enough food to sustain my body, and enough money to meet my monthly expenses. I was blessed with a supportive extended family and friends in abundance. I found some comfort in knowing that Bert was in heaven, watching over us and no longer suffering from whatever issues had caused his unbearable depression.

Still . . . what I wanted to do and what I actually accomplished were worlds apart. I was weak-willed. Too physically and mentally weary on most days, I had no choice but to be patient and wait to see what each new day would bring. I reminded myself that God works in His own time, because He knows what's best for us. He knows how those of us who are left behind to grieve over our loss lose our grip on the already fragile sanity we possess while on this earth. Times of trial reveal exactly how "human" we are. God's ways are not our ways. Our brains cannot fully comprehend His ways. We get stuck on our limited understanding.

As my first summer without Bert progressed, I continued to cry out, as did Job and millions of Christians throughout the centuries, *why is God silent?* Why didn't God speak to Bert in time to prevent his death? Why didn't He warn one of us who loved him of his depression and need for help? Why doesn't God stop all the suffering of those of us who were left behind? If He isn't turning a blind eye to our struggles, then what is He doing? Why doesn't He swoop down or send one of His angels to help us through our everyday existence? Why doesn't He immediately show us how to deal with our great sorrow?

In the darkness and in the silence of my journey toward the unknown, I continued to trust Him. Like Job, I said, *"Though he slay me, yet will I hope in him . . ."* (Job 13:15) And so I asked the *whys* for weeks and months, while I dealt with the nonstop memories that seemed to prolong my recovery and the mayhem of seemingly endless tasks that required tending yesterday. Although God's answers weren't coming on my timetable, I had faith they would come.

And after you have suffered a little while, the God of all grace, who has called you to his eternal glory in Christ, will himself restore, confirm, strengthen, and establish you.
— 1 Peter 5:10 (ESV)

Rejoice in hope, be patient in tribulation, be constant in prayer . . .
— Romans 12:12 (ESV)

Chapter 7

Lingering Doubts

By the time I entered the fourth month, I was still a confused suicide survivor who felt woefully inadequate to deal with any hiccup. I was, however, ready to acknowledge I had no choice other than to put one foot in front of the other and plod from one difficulty to the next. Bert was dead and gone. I was once again the breadwinner of the family. The head of the household. It was my responsibility to make decisions, pay bills, keep up the house and property, and tend to all the daily chores involving meals, laundry, and cars.

I hated being a widow. I hadn't asked for the role. I had not been given even one lousy hour to prepare for it. Twelve weeks had passed and nothing was getting easier. I found this revelation depressing.

Chris and Emily were busy with their respective school activities and needed me less often. Chris lived close to the campus, but he called me often. I didn't want to lie about how I was doing, so I quickly turned our conversations to topics concerning his new friends, sports, his classes and professors. Emily focused on her studies, cheerleading practice, and going to the games with her friends on the squad. As much as I could, I attended the games to applaud her performance from the bleachers, all the while missing Bert's enthusiastic shouts of approval by my side. I could tell both children were still dealing with their own grief, but because of their changed schedules, we had decided to discontinue our one-on-one sessions with the bereavement therapist. I was also concerned about the financial burden of such therapy. Medical insurance didn't pay for it, and three cash payments for individual hour-long talks took a large chunk from our greatly tightened household budget. It needed to go toward school expenses. That was another burden suicide survivors face, but not planned for in their budgets . . . and another reason why having the Great Healer as our therapist on call at all hours of the day and night is so wonderful. His services are free of charge.

I spent much of my "alone" time writing in my journal and attempting to reevaluate not only my marriage, but my whole life. Time and again, I was haunted by thoughts that I hadn't really known Bert. He had kept things to himself. Secrets. He had pasted smiles on his face and pretended everything was all right, all the while being cheerful, thoughtful, selfless . . . and secretive. For some reason, he had made the choice not to share his feelings, his worries, his business concerns and setbacks. It was easy for him to maintain this façade of optimism because he spent five days of every week miles away from home. He didn't have to face me or fear I'd catch him in a lie. Yes, a lie. Because everything was *not* okay.

I seemed to have no power over my wildly vacillating emotions. I remembered the stories others in the support group had told of how their emotions controlled their lives. They would often snap at people when this wasn't their normal demeanor, and either be unusually vivacious or uncommonly moody and quiet. They would experience bouts of deep anger at the loved one who had taken his or her life, and then suffer days of guilt over harboring such thoughts. I seemed to be following this pattern. I found myself resenting Bert and his secrets, being furious that he so cavalierly chose to end his life without giving me even a hint of his intentions, and then feeling remorse over my deep-felt bitterness.

There were days when I worked zealously to reconstruct every minute of the weeks preceding the suicide. I struggled to remember every word of each conversation, looking for clues, trying to rationalize my failure to identify exactly when Bert had changed and what had triggered the change. No matter how often I reminded myself that Bert's choices were not mine and I had no control over how he or anyone chose to think and act, I continued to accept the blame for his final choice. Never mind that he had excluded me from any decision that might have altered the course of his future . . . and mine. Then when I thought of how our last several conversations had been based on a cover-up, I was hurt all over again. Bert had let me chat away about nonsensical, trivial things, about upcoming events, about family dilemmas and mounting expenses, and about how much I looked forward to weekends and having him home with me, without sharing much of his own work-week activities. Maybe he had been waiting for me to ask more detailed questions, to stop assuming everything was fine.

I had failed him.

No matter how deeply I delved into memories, I couldn't wrap my head around what had prompted Bert's depression and how he was able to hide it from me. Ironically, we had both seen our family doctor for complete physicals only a month before the suicide and received "a clean bill of health." Of course, when a doctor asks pointed questions concerning symptoms caused by stress, we had the choice to confide or merely shrug and say "everything is fine." That's what Bert said. "Everything is fine, doc." I'm not a doctor. I'm not a therapist. I had no experience with depression. I didn't know the symptoms, so I couldn't say, "That's not true."

Bert had failed me.

And so, with this line of thinking, I'd do a complete flip and become defensive. The suicide wasn't my fault after all. It was Bert's fault. He had chosen to remain mute. He had chosen to take the most drastic sort of "cure" for what ailed him. Self-murder. Then I immediately brushed such horrible thoughts from my mind. They in no way suited the man I had loved and respected and married. He was brave and intelligent and hardworking and . . . .

As I bounced from one emotional spectrum to the next, I did make one resolution. I resolved to be totally honest with my children and my extended family members. No more games. Not any more. Through this painful experience, I finally understood the importance of being forthright, even if it temporarily caused disappointment, frustration, or even anger. The days of pretending were over. I'd played games with everyone, including Bert. I was the nice wife, the nice mother, the nice daughter and sister. Because I genuinely cared about the feelings of everyone, I habitually swallowed my often differing opinions and said what I thought they wanted to hear. That's what Bert had done with me and with everyone else in the family. He was what we expected and wanted him to be. He had said what he thought we wanted to hear. Ask Bert. He'll know what to do.

But he hadn't felt comfortable sharing his burdens with any of us, especially not with me.

Throughout the weeks of my ongoing personal grieving, I chastised myself often for professing to believe God was actively engaged in guiding me through the dark tunnel of despair toward the light, but then not letting go of my resentments. I was still sick at heart. I wanted to touch the hem of His garment and be instantly healed, like so many who had experienced miracles during Jesus' time on earth. I wanted immediate relief of my pain. On the spot proof that my cries for help were heard. I wanted to write the script and direct the recovery process.

But God doesn't work that way. Since He alone is omnipotent and omniscient, I had to trust that He knew the best time for each step of my journey back to the life He wanted me to enjoy. In my daily devotions, I felt shame for the way I had behaved upon hearing of Bert's suicide, especially for the message it projected to my children and others in the family. What kind of example was I to decide life wasn't worth living without one specific person I loved in it? I was surrounded by those who loved me. I was not alone. Rather than wishing I were dead, or wishing I could die, and even thinking about how I could go through with my own suicide, I should have fallen to my knees and quietly sought God's wisdom.

Fortunately, God knows about the frailty of the human spirit and isn't shocked by our sagging faith. He doesn't turn aside in disgust and leave us to our own misery. He waits and watches and sends word to us through others whose faith is stronger at the time. He provides enlightenment through the voices of those who wrote the Gospels. He guides us to the right sentences in the right books and speaks loudly enough to be heard. Ralph Waldo Emerson wrote, "When it is dark enough, you can see the stars." By the end of the fourth month as a bereaved widow, I was beginning to see a few. Friedrich Nietzsche wrote, "He who has a *why* to live can bear almost any *how*." I had an infinite number of *whys* and believed that God would tell me *how* to live without Bert. Adversity introduces us to ourselves. I was having a cold, hard look at myself and knew it was time to start practicing what I believed.

In the next couple of weeks, I was able to project to my children my restored belief that God was in control. He was in us and beside us and always speaking to us in his Word . . . the holy Bible. We would get through our grieving for Bert eventually. Our faith would sustain us.

"We're the lucky ones," I told them. "Our healing will be much quicker and more complete than for those who are suffering from similar circumstances but lack any belief in a loving God. Those who don't believe God allowed his Son to be crucified in order to save us for all eternity have nothing but their inadequate experiences and the platitudes of friends to bring them comfort. Just think, many of them will feel nothing but emptiness the rest of their lives. Soul-destroying, life-killing emptiness. I don't believe our human minds are able to conjure up any sustaining degree of reassurance there will be a happy future for us. No painless rationale for how to survive the suicide of our loved one either. They can't rest their hope on any thought of heaven or eternity with their loved one, like we can."

I reminded them of our journey through these first difficult months. "We've sought group support and had individual therapy with a medical specialist, but all three of us learned that no recital of facts and figures or recounting of other people's experiences with suicide have brought us personal consolation. It only served to transmit the message that suffering is supposedly 'normal' after such a tragedy. At the same time, kids, our efforts were beneficial in that they reminded us that as human beings we're terribly flawed and limited in what we can do on our own. I don't know about you, but I'm thankful to know that Bert is in heaven and no longer tormented by whatever drove him to take such an irreversible act. We'll join him some day and live for eternity in utter contentment. I would much, much rather believe that than believe in nothing."

A friend recommended an old book to me: *The Color of Night*, written in 1977 (Augsburg Publishing). Gerhard Frost, the author, reflected on the life and sufferings of Job, who "wrestled with the difficult issues we face during times of crisis, such as trust in God, the meaning of life, and unfairness in the world." He wrote that Job's outcry was more than a complaint against the agony of isolation and the loss of his supporting community. It was even above the *whys* of a suffering human being, like those of us in Bert's family. It was more of "a religious outcry, a protest against life's unyielding absurdity, against the incoherence of his situation."

Every morning upon awakening, I would make my coffee and begin reading my Bible. To me, there was no better way to start the day. There were many times I didn't quite understand what I was reading, but it didn't matter. I read anyway. Usually, God would lead me to a particular verse that spoke directly to me and gave me something to think about during the long hours of the day. After reading, I would move on to my prayers and meditation. I talked with God and told Him about my many worries and concerns. Many times, I didn't even have to put words to my feelings. I knew God was reading my mind and knew what was in my heart. He had created me and knew me better than I knew myself. I'd sit in the silence and try to hear what He wanted me to know. Any thought that came to my mind was His voice through the Holy Spirit talking to me. I listened. I asked for guidance and protection and comfort. I asked for the wisdom to know what to do for my children, my parents, Bert's parents, and with the rest of my life. I also asked God for His forgiveness of my doubts and lamentations over having to endure such pain and sorrow after Bert's death. I asked Him to fill my heart with an everlasting supply of faith and hope.

I asked Him for understanding of "the incoherence of his situation."

As I looked back over the course of my life, I realized that God would never have allowed the loss of something I thought necessary from my life without bringing something special in return. I would need to wait with great patience and expectation. God would not disappoint me.

During these quiet times, I would talk with Bert as well, as though he were sitting next to me. I believed he was watching over the children and me and that he had a hand in directing our lives. Many times, I was certain he had left clues in my pathway to help me to get to where I needed to go.

It was during this month that I finally began to dream. I knew that dreams only come when we're in our deepest sleep and my nights to date had been fitful for so long I had never reached that level. Now I would awaken knowing I had dreamt about something. Usually I couldn't remember the dream, but I looked forward to the time when I would. Finally there were nights when I didn't need a sleeping pill. I could fall asleep naturally and know that God was bringing me the rest and rejuvenation I needed. I knew that even though I didn't remember my dreams, any message being sent to me would be stored in my subconscious mind, and perhaps I would be able to apply what I'd worked out later.

Gradually I began to see Bert in my dreams and remember them upon waking. One of the first things I noticed was that he acted as though he weren't dead, which of course he wasn't. He was "alive" as a new creature in his heavenly body, as the Bible states. I wondered if he was trying to tell me something important. Another repeated dream had me persistently trying to reach him by phone. Either that, or he would be calling me. What was he trying to communicate?

One day I had the urge to call Noe, Bert's best friend. We had called each other from time to time over the past several weeks to see how the other was doing, but this time I wanted to tell him about my dreams. "Noe, I keep having the same dream. That Bert is trying to reach me by phone, but I can't figure out the message he's conveying. I wake up without hearing him tell me."

"That is so weird, Letty," he said. "I had a dream a couple of nights ago that Bert called and wanted me to tell you not to worry about anything. He said everything was going to be okay. He wanted me to get that message to you."

Neither of us knew what to do about it, but it made us more confident in our faith that there was a heaven and Bert was with God and looking out for us.

One night, after that, I had a particularly unsettling dream. We were at the ranch and Bert began talking about his death. "Someone shot me,

Letty, but I don't want you to tell anyone." He gave no reason why I should keep this to myself. I began to sob in my dream. I woke up and realized I was crying in reality. Deeply disturbed, I cried out to God. "Have we been terribly wrong all this time? Have we believed this unspeakable tragedy, without delving into it more deeply? Dear God, tell me what to do! Maybe Bert didn't take his life after all. *Maybe someone did kill him.*"

I thought of my long conversations with his sister, Lisa, who lives in Arizona. Once a police officer, she had dealt with several suicides while actively serving in the department. We admitted to each other that we had been having persistent reservations about the ruling of Bert's death. It seemed too easy. Neither of us wholly believed that Bert would ever take such a drastic action without first revealing the depth of his depression or problems leading up to that day.

Now, as soon as the sun rose and I adjusted the time for the Mountain Standard Zone — one hour earlier than in San Antonio — I called Lisa and told her about my dream. "I don't know if I'm slipping back into denial or it's just plain wishful thinking, Lisa, but this dream was so clear and so definitive, I'm seriously questioning whether Bert took his life."

"I feel the same way, Letty. I've been going over and over the police report in detail and believing more often that something just doesn't make sense."

The official ruling of Bert's death was suicide, but the sketchy reports were bringing a host of doubts about the verdict. Bert was not the kind of person who would take his life. He was a man of great faith. He was a family man who cared deeply about our well-being. How awful for all of us to believe he would make such a choice, when perhaps he hadn't. And if he hadn't, that meant he had been murdered. Shouldn't the truth be made known?

My conversation with Lisa brought back all my original questions. Had he been attacked by one or more people? Were they illegal aliens after his cattle? The ranch wasn't far from the border between Mexico and the United States. Had he suffered? Had he fought back, before the fatal shot? Is that why he hadn't left a note or said final words of love to me?

83

The questions came in a fury and left me feeling bereft. Lisa and I decided that in order to have some kind of closure, we would have to seek answers to our questions from those who had made the report. We knew what we had to do.

Lisa called the investigator in Laredo and set up an appointment for us to meet with him. We told ourselves the trip wouldn't be wasted, because the police still had some of Bert's personal belongings and the weapon that was used for the killing. They could now be returned to our custody. It was critical that our lingering doubts be put to rest.

Therefore, I tell you, whatever you ask for in prayer, believe that you have received it, and it will be yours.
— Mark 11:24

Trust me in your times of trouble, and I will rescue you, and you will give me glory. — Psalm 50:15 (NLT)

Chapter 8

Truth and Trust

The night before our scheduled departure I had a panic attack. Although I had been preparing myself for the trip to Laredo for a couple of weeks, I experienced a sudden sense of terror. My heart raced out of control and I felt weak and faint, like I was losing control of my body. As the seconds progressed, I gasped for air and had to sit down, clutching my chest. I knew I was in a state of panic, but I convinced myself I was having a heart attack. I shook my hands to make the tingling go away.

For several days, I had been feeling increasingly more overwhelmed by the thought that my beloved Bert had been murdered. I was scared. What if this were true? I had become angry with myself for not taking action sooner. I should have launched an investigation immediately after the funeral. I should have made the trip to Laredo to ferret out the truth. I should have immediately rejected the very notion of Bert's resorting to suicide to solve a problem.

Although I spent too much time each day crying and wringing my hands, as though in a returned state of helplessness, I felt I was in control. I had methodically gathered papers I might need to show the investigators, tended to chores around the house, and kept in contact with Emily and Chris to let them know why I felt the trip was necessary. Each day, the tension built, but I had felt perfectly capable of dealing with it.

Now I was suffering an unexpected setback.

Fortunately, panic attacks don't linger. They come and they go. Within the hour, with focused attention on taking deep breaths and letting them out slowly, my breathing returned to normal, the racing palpitations of my heart slowed, and I could go about my final preparations. But the episode was a reminder that my ordeal was not over. I still had a long way to go.

Early the next morning, I drove to my in-laws to pick up Lisa. Bert's parents were somewhat hesitant and fearful about us taking such a stressful trip by ourselves, but they were also resigned to the fact that we intended to go through with it no matter what. "You have our blessing," my father-in-law said. "Drive safely and come home soon. Call us, when you find out something, one way or the other. Our thoughts will be with you."

While driving to Laredo, Lisa and I talked about Bert. We laughed and cried over many shared memories of him, and we listened to the CD containing the music played at the Rosary. We were finally able to listen to the words of the songs, as we hadn't heard them that night when our hearts were breaking and our minds were leaping from one thought to the other in the first phase of our denial.

Later, as we rested in the hotel room the evening before the meeting with the Laredo police investigation officer, we got to know each other even better. Until now, I really hadn't known Lisa well, as she lived so far away. Since the day after Bert's death, when our first of many conversations had taken place, we had grown closer and soon felt as if we had known each other all our lives. We were very much alike. While sitting cross-legged on the hotel bed, I made a confession. "Bert and I stayed at this hotel so many times, Lisa. We loved it here. In fact, we probably stayed in this very room." I peered wistfully about the room, glad I had someone to share the moment with who could understand my emotional strain.

For the next couple of hours we organized our thoughts for the meeting by writing down all the questions that had been going through our minds the past few weeks. We had no expectations. We didn't know anything about the investigator or how he would handle our inquiries. All we knew was that we felt strongly we were being led by God to go forward with this exploration.

Upon awakening, we prepared ourselves physically, emotionally, and spiritually. It was our intention to drive to the ranch after meeting with the officials in the sheriff's department, and spend the night at our house. Lisa had never been there, and I hadn't made the visit since Bert's death. I was dreading that part of our trip, but at the same time I wanted to get it over with.

Before leaving the hotel, we held hands and prayed. "Our dear loving Father, please be with us as we move forward in this very difficult part of our journey toward restored wholeness. Protect us both physically and mentally, as we seek the truth. Give us the courage and the strength to move forward with reasonableness and not emotional defiance. Give us the questions to ask. Reveal to us what we need to know, to put our hearts and minds to rest and come to closure. Help as we wrestle with the truth and show us how to accept it, whatever it may be. We believe you have led us to make this trip. In Jesus name we pray. Amen."

There was no denying our anxiety. This was no ordinary activity. Even while our heartfelt belief was that Bert couldn't possibly have taken his life, we knew it was feasible. We both believed that when we finally left the sheriff's office, we would be convinced one way or the other.

After arriving at the designated building and introducing ourselves, we were led to a conference room and seated at a round conference table. We were served coffee and within a few minutes, the investigator entered the room, introduced himself, and then patiently answered our questions.

I was the first to speak, and I was startled at the sound of my shaking voice. "My brother-in-law told me that when he picked up Bert's truck at . . . at the place where you impound vehicles, all of the soiled clothes that he kept in a laundry bag to take to the cleaners were scattered throughout the back seat. Bert would never have done that. He was a very neat person; he liked everything tidy. Is . . . is that the way you found them, or did your people do that during their investigation? Should we wonder who did this or why they were found in that way?"

The man didn't flinch at my question. "It's part of our procedure to go through containers of any kind to look for clues that might help us decide whether the death of the individual was self-inflicted or due to a crime. It's very likely that one of my team sorted through the bag of laundry. Leaving it scattered and unpacked let others know it had already been examined. That's why we don't take the time to put things back as found."

"Did you see any other tire marks on the ground near or around his truck to show another vehicle had been present that morning?"

"No, ma'am, I'm sorry, we didn't."

My questioning continued along this line. Because of Lisa's work as a police officer, she was more familiar with the specifics concerning the position of Bert's body, the entrance and exit of the bullet, fingerprints, and gunpowder residue. She asked several questions and received direct replies to them all. I didn't fully understand the scope of this conversation, but trusted that she did. I watched her facial expressions to determine if she believed the answers. It became clear to me that the police had been thorough in their investigation, and their evidence showed Bert had, indeed, committed self-murder; no one else had caused his death.

My heart sank. Truthfully? I had hoped for another possibility . . . one that was still horrific in scope but would be easier to accept. Then my self-blame could end. My condemnation of Bert's decision could end. My sense of shame and guilt could end. Murder or death by natural causes is difficult, but much easier for survivors to accept.

At that point, an officer brought in two boxes containing Bert's personal belongings. The first one included his cellphone, wallet, watch, a few keys, and other items I can't remember right now. Then we were presented with the second sealed box containing Bert's gun — the one he had used to take his life. The last thing he had held in his hand.

"If you decide you'd rather not take the weapon back to San Antonio with you, our procedure is to lock it in the vault until it is finally destroyed," the investigator said. "And just to let you know, ladies, the weapon is in the same condition in which it was recovered. It has never been cleaned. I'm telling you this, in case you should decide not to take a look at it."

He knew by the look on our faces that the very thought of seeing blood or other body parts shocked us. As he rose to his feet, he added, "I'll leave you alone to talk about what you want to do."

Lisa and I watched him exit the room and close the door behind him. With tears filling our eyes, we stared silently at each other and then at the box on the table. "Lisa," I finally said, when I'd found my voice, "what do you think about everything we've been told? Have we been given the run-around, because we're women and easily swayed when we're in such turmoil mentally? Was the investigation thorough?"

"I believe him, Letty. I don't think he was lying about anything."

"He did it, didn't he? Bert pulled the trigger on his own gun. He took his life. He wasn't murdered." I stared at the sealed box again. "Why take the weapon home? What good would it do any of us? I— I have no desire to see it. *Not ever.*" I placed my arms on the table to cradle my head and sobbed.

Lisa touched my hair. "Everything is going to be okay again, Letty. This is the reason we came down here. Remember? We prayed that whatever we needed to know would be revealed. We knew that after having our questions answered, we would know the truth. Now we know. The truth is hard to hear, but we'll deal with it, with God's help."

Just then the investigator returned. Before he even had a chance to speak, Lisa said, "We've decided we don't want to take possession of the gun. We'd like you to destroy it."

He nodded. "I understand, and I'm so sorry. I wish I could have provided a different outcome for you."

As we drove away from the building, we were silent for a long while. Struggling with a fresh flood of tears and an overwhelming wave of vulnerability, I turned to Lisa. "I— I feel as though I just found out the terrible news for the first time."

"I know, I feel the same way. It seems like any progress we've made in these last few months has been completely erased, like we've been in a time warp. We're back to square one." I couldn't face the thought of having to start my grieving process all over again. Yes, the investigator had answered all our questions. Yet the one question that would remain a mystery forever, the one question neither he nor anyone could ever answer was *why*? The closure we so desperately wanted was pushed farther into the future

Suddenly, I remembered that Noe had also planned to drive to Laredo; we were to meet him for lunch to talk about our meeting. If Lisa and I decided it was necessary, he had volunteered to accompany us to our house located on my family's ranch which had been named after my grandfather, Pedro Leal. I called Noe on my cellphone and learned he had just arrived in town. "Meet us at that taco café where we've eaten so many times before, Noe. We'll wait for you outside at one of the picnic tables."

Hearing his voice over the phone stirred my ready-to-explode emotions and I struggled to control them. Knowing I was to see one of Bert's best friends was bringing back a deluge of memories. Despite my intentions to maintain decorum, as soon as Noe strolled onto the patio, my reaction was as it had been on May the 6th. Bert was gone. We'd never spend time in Laredo together again. He'd never raise cattle. He'd never barbecue a side of beef for our family and friends at our home. I threw my arms around Noe and cried all over again. *"He did it. He killed himself. He wasn't murdered. Why did he do it, Noe? Tell me why!"*

Noe just shook his head. What could he say? "I'm sorry, Letty. We have to accept it and go on. I'm sorry. I'm so sorry."

When I regained my composure, we sat at the picnic table and talked. Lisa filled him in on everything we had learned as I stared blankly into space, once more experiencing the full impact of shock. Sometime later, Lisa and I headed for the ranch. The plan was to spend the rest of the day and night there and return to San Antonio the following morning.

Driving in a mental fog, I veered onto the dirt road leading to our ranch house, my heart thudding in my chest and my hands trembling on the wheel. I was terrified. No amount of deep breathing or trying to deflect my thoughts toward mundane things was effective. I dreaded the ordeal to come. I was tired of crying, tired of feeling I had no ability to control my responses to events, tired of feeling the pain of loss. But this was *our* ranch house. We had built it together. I had no desire to set foot on the property. It meant nothing to me without Bert there to enjoy the vast expanse of brush-filled land that made a perfect deer-hunting site and serene getaway from city life.

As I parked the car next to the house, Lisa turned to me. "Do you want me to give you time to yourself? Should I stay out here, while you go inside?"

"No, no. I want you with me. Just prepare yourself. I'm not sure if I'm going to be able to do this."

We walked up the three steps leading to the porch. I placed my hand on the doorknob and turned it slowly, filled with a suffocating feeling of intense trepidation. As I opened the door, the first thing I noticed were the camouflage overalls Bert had used during the winter months when he went hunting. They were hanging on the hat rack. Choking on my tears, I rushed forward to embrace them, wishing Bert's sturdy body was in them. My tears flowed steadily and I cried for what seemed like hours. That's all it took to break the emotional dam that allowed me to move forward one step at a time. Camouflage overalls. How could I get through the next hours? Bert's presence permeated every room. I pictured him sitting in his favorite chair. I heard his voice in the kitchen asking if I wanted coffee. I saw him in framed pictures and remembered the occasion when each was taken.

Finally, weak and physically exhausted, I slumped lifeless onto the couch. Once again, my thoughts dived headlong into the murky waters of personal defeat. I didn't have the energy or the desire to go on living. Deep in my own misery, I almost missed hearing the sounds of Lisa stirring nearby. I glanced at her and was instantly ashamed that I had conducted another personal pity party without once thinking of her pain. "I'm so sorry, Lisa. I'm so sorry. This is hard for you, too. Whatever are we going to do? Why isn't believing that God will heal me enough? Why can't I accept that life for everyone is rife with trials and suffering, not only mine? Why can't I stop all this . . . this incessant weeping? It doesn't change anything. It doesn't turn back the clock. It's . . . it's just an energy-draining waste of time. I'm so scared I'm going to be like some of those people in the support group I attended, Lisa. They had been attending meetings monthly for several years. *Years!* Some quit and then returned when their repressed feelings returned. Are we going to live like . . . like *this* the rest of our lives?" I threw up my arms in frustration.

Lisa shrugged. She knew implicitly there was nothing she could say to soothe my grieving spirit, but she tried anyway. "You've done what you needed to do as Bert's wife, Letty. You spoke with the authorities. You learned the truth, so you don't need to rely on your imagination anymore. You have now returned to the ranch home you once shared . . . and you've survived."

So . . . then came the calm after the storm. I spent considerable time simply walking throughout the rooms of the house. Everything I saw, smelled, and touched held special memories. Later, with the help of my brother Pete, my sister-in-law Loressa, and my cousins, I found myself relaxing and even enjoying the ranch, especially while in their company, just as I knew Bert would have wanted me to do. My cousins had planned a barbeque for us. We sat around the campfire and talked about Bert. Of all the places in the world he'd visited, he loved the ranch the most. He was no longer there to share it with us, but we felt his presence.

On our return trip to San Antonio, Lisa and I didn't talk much at first. We were absorbing what our hearts and minds had experienced during those difficult two days. Unexpectedly, Bert's sister began to cry. Finally, her remarkably stiff upper lip had fallen victim to her inner turmoil. I knew it was my turn to comfort her and pulled over to the side of the road so I could give her all my attention.

"Letty," she said, crying uncontrollably, "I feel so guilty. I feel as if we left Bert behind. We're going back home and . . . and he's still *there*."

I hugged her tightly. "Oh, Lisa, you know how much he loved the ranch. If we left his spirit there, it's exactly where he'd want to be. But he's not just there; he's everywhere in our hearts. No matter where we are, we'll have Bert with us, for the rest of our lives."

Going to the ranch had been a big step for me. I was grateful to everyone who supported me in that difficult test. It had also been a tough test for Lisa. We had accomplished what we set out to do. Rationally, I could now accept the truth; at times, I could even talk about it in clear tones without crying. But despite all my good intentions, despite the strengthening of my faith in God's abiding love and presence in my life, despite what I wanted to do and think and believe, my subconscious mind took its own path, leading me right back into the pits of despair again. Because I had allowed myself to believe someone else was responsible for Bert's death, because I so desperately needed to fix the blame on someone other than him or me . . . I now found myself starting the grieving process all over again.

I was no different from all those people at the support group after all, and no different from those who had related their stories in the secular books I'd read about how they had been unable to deal with the shock of their loved one's suicide. Once again, I felt a growing sense of anger. Anger at Bert for leaving me without a single written word of explanation, anger at God for what He could've prevented, and anger at myself for not realizing what a dark place Bert must've been in. Anger at life in general. It wasn't fair. It wasn't orderly. Then filled with guilt, I'd pray all the harder for God to forgive me for this misplaced anger and to replace it with peace of mind and purpose. The work ahead of me seemed like an immovable mountain. But God has said we *can* move mountains, when our faith is strong enough. *". . . For truly, I say to you, if you have faith like a grain of mustard seed, you will say to this mountain, 'Move from here to there,' and it will move, and nothing will be impossible for you."* (Matthew 17:20)

I especially prayed for the ability to forgive Bert. Unless I was able to forgive him, I would never heal. God promises to do for us what we can't do for ourselves. I needed Him now more than ever before. I needed Him to help me forgive anyone and everyone who may have played a part in producing the pressure that finally broke Bert's spirit and will to live.

A few days after my trip to Laredo, I visited the cemetery. As I sat on a bench overlooking Bert's grave, I thought about his funeral and burial services. With fresh tears streaming down my cheeks, I talked to him. Six months had passed since I last held him in my arms and said goodbye for what I thought was only a few days. Death comes without warning. Too many of us are left thinking "If only I'd known, then I'd have . . . ." I thought of something I'd read recently. Marcel Proust, an early 1900's French novelist, wrote, "We say that the hour of death cannot be forecast, but when we say this, we imagine that hour as placed in an obscure and distant future. It never occurs to us that it has any connection with the day already begun or that death could arrive this same afternoon, this afternoon which is so certain and which has every hour filled in advance." I hadn't known when I kissed Bert goodbye that early Tuesday morning that it would be the last time our lips would touch in an expression of our love.

Looking around, I noticed an elderly man with his little dog at the site of where his loved one had been buried. I wondered if the deceased was his wife, or perhaps his parents or a child. It didn't matter; it was obvious to me by his demeanor that it was someone he'd loved. I felt his sorrow. I understood how bereft he felt and how difficult and pointless his life seemed at times. As I watched him, I prayed that God would bring him comfort. I wondered how long he'd been grieving. He looked so sad. He called to his dog and they trudged across the grassy knoll to his car. Would he return the next day or the next week? Did he have a schedule? Had he been visiting the grave to mourn and remember happier times for months . . . or years? Once I was back in my car, I realized the gentleman must have been wondering the same things about me.

That night I dreamed that every time I was driving my car to some unnamed destination I would black out. When I "awoke" from this temporary blackout, I would find myself on the other side of town with no memory of how I had gotten there. At first, there was considerable traffic. I would have trouble with my car and I was afraid I wouldn't survive the commotion. Miraculously, I ended up at the church I used to attend as a child. It is far from where I live now. All I remember is being in the dark and then arriving at the church. Upon awakening the next morning, I attempted to remember the details of the dream and to interpret what it meant. I could only conclude that although I was often "in the dark" concerning the whys of my current travails, God was guiding me. I might not be able to see, because I was traveling blind, but I needed to have faith that God is "the way, the truth, and the light."

On November the 18th, I awoke to remember it was my 48th birthday. I would mark the day without Bert's gifts and good wishes. The thought occurred to me that Bert would always remain age 41. I thought of how Marilyn Monroe and Princess Diana are remembered as they were at the time of their deaths — forever young and beautiful — and wondered how this would affect my memories of Bert as I continued to age. I was already six years older than he when we married. Then I thought of how we picture our Lord . . . only 33 when He was crucified on the cross. Age has no meaning in heaven. We will take on a heavenly appearance and live forever with no thoughts of aging or the acquiring of wrinkles or infirmities. Our personal trials and suffering will come to an end. I quietly thanked God for my life, for my health and for His countless blessings. I prayed that He'd give me the wisdom to make better, wiser decisions in the year to come, especially those that could affect the lives of those I loved. I prayed for the courage and strength to bear the pain that came with my grieving for Bert with even a modicum of the grace He had shown while willingly suffering to provide an easier way for me to spend eternity with Him. All I had to do was believe in Him and ask for His forgiveness. I could do nothing to earn this gift . . . the greatest birthday gift I could ever receive from anyone. I didn't need anything else.

Armed with the truth of my husband's shocking death, I once again put all my trust in the Lord. Only He could bring me the peace I needed to become all He wanted me to be in the upcoming year.

Trust in the Lord with all your heart and lean not on your own understanding; in all your ways acknowledge him, and he will make your paths straight. — Proverbs 3:5-6 (NIV)

If any of you is lacking in wisdom, ask God, who gives to all generously and ungrudgingly, and it will be given you. But ask in faith, never doubting, for the one who doubts is like a wave of the sea, driven and tossed by the wind. — James 1:5-6 (NIV)

Chapter 9

Coping with Celebrations

Although the holidays of Thanksgiving and Christmas were several weeks ahead of me, I started to feel the undercurrents of apprehensiveness. The holidays were special in a family as large as ours. Bert and I had several siblings each and everyone enjoyed the round of family dinners, open houses, and barbeques that defined our growing relationships. How could I possibly participate this year?

No matter how the other members of Bert's family pretended to be "fine," each of us was having difficulty dealing with the circumstances of Bert's death. If he had been killed in the line of duty as a soldier or officer of the law, if he had been the victim of a senseless car accident, or if he died of cancer or an unexpected heart attack, we would still be grieving over his loss in our family circle, but with greater understanding of life's misfortunes. But none of these formed the scenario we were handed. Bert had chosen to withdraw from us. He had confided in no one. We were all still reeling from his decision. Bert had been an integral part of our family celebrations. How could we express our thankfulness to God for another year of bountiful blessings, when we were feeling left out of them?

Unexpectedly, I received an invitation from my church about a grief support group being organized specifically for those who had recently lost a loved one and shared my same concern — how to get through the holidays. Meetings would be held once a week for six weeks. It was another answer to prayer and exactly what I needed. I made the decision to attend and extended the invitation to Bert's sister Pearl.

Those six weeks were difficult but helpful. There is a special kind of comfort that comes from those who have lost loved ones, regardless of the circumstances or the length of time since their parting. Some attendees were new survivors and others had suffered their loss years ago. The reality was stark that my life would always be different and difficult. I would never fully "get over it," but, with God's help, I would eventually learn to live with the truth of my loss.

Despite our being complete strangers, we had one important thing in common that had not been a part of the first support group I attended: we believed wholeheartedly in a loving and caring God who provided whatever comfort and strength we required on a daily basis. Without a belief in His promise of an eternal life with our loved ones, life held no meaning. During our meetings, I shared the small gains I had made in my grieving process because of my daily talks with God, and I welcomed whatever knowledge and inspiration had come to other participants during their own journey. We agreed that the progression toward wholeness of spirit was painfully slow, and our humanness too often got in the way of our full acceptance of God's grace. Without it, however, we would likely become recluses, unable to function with any sense of purpose. We leaned on the truth of God's promise in II Corinthians 12:9: *"My grace is sufficient for you, for My strength is made perfect in weakness."*

We were instructed to bring a picture of our loved one to our last meeting before the Thanksgiving holiday. We shared them and talked a bit about the happy things we remembered about their participation in these special family events. Some spoke about the favorite traditional meal or dessert of their husband or son, or about their most memorable gift from them. Some stories brought laughter, some tears. When it was my turn, I realized I was speaking of Bert in the past tense, a reminder of the truth that he was gone forever, except in my memory. It was another step forward for me.

On November 2nd, my church celebrated a special All Souls' Day requiem mass for loved ones who had faithfully departed. I was comforted by the presence of my siblings and their spouses and also the people I had met at the support group who attended the service with their families. It was a solemn and beautiful commemoration, with prayers and music that fed our souls and filled us with love and compassion for each other. While listening to the priest, my thoughts drifted from a focus on Bert to the others I'd known in my lifetime who had also passed from their earthly life. My tears flowed freely, but this time it wasn't from a sense of depression or frustration or anger. It was from thankfulness to God for the lives of these special people who had enriched my life. I thanked Him again for the remarkable love He had shown in sending His Son to die for my sins so that I didn't have to make personal sacrifices to earn my way into heaven. His gift ensured I would spend eternity with my loved ones in heaven and, especially, that I would one day see Bert again.

While friends, family, and neighbors were making plans for the upcoming holidays, it often bothered me that they were able to look forward to them without the dread I was experiencing. They seemed to be avoiding any discussion of how I was coping with the festivities without Bert, and I wanted to talk about him. Then I'd remind myself they were doing exactly what they should be doing for the sake of their own family members. Bert was my husband, not theirs.

It bothered me, too, that despite every positive experience in church or in my private devotions, and with every revelation that God was in charge, and regardless of my understanding the importance for me to be a strong witness of my faith to others — especially to my children and other family members — *I wasn't being that.* I seemed to want to hang onto my sadness. I hated the feeling and was ashamed of my thoughts. Finally, I took a long, hard look in the mirror and admitted the truth. As long as I remained morose and listless, I wouldn't be expected to participate. I didn't want to pretend I looked forward to shopping and gift wrapping, singing Christmas carols, or baking special cookies. Surely no one expected me to be the jovial, ever-sociable woman of the previous year, but as a Christian I should be able to live what I believed. Nevertheless, I became overly sensitive and found myself easily hurt by some of the comments others made. When someone said, "He's gone now," the bluntness of the comment felt more like a sharp stab. I didn't like it. It was all right for me to voice that fact, but not someone else. It seemed so dismissive. Like Bert was no longer important. My feelings were no longer important.

Despite the passage of six months, I was still struggling with not being one part of a two-member team. Whenever a decision was required, I felt as though I needed to first seek Bert's approval. I would catch myself thinking, "What would Bert do?" or "Would Bert approve of what I'm about to do? Would his feelings be hurt if I attend the party without him? Am I laughing too hard, too long? Am I being disrespectful?" It was as if my trying to move forward meant my love for him had to diminish, or that my making an independent decision meant I was being disloyal to him. I remembered the saying, "Out of sight, out of mind." I didn't want my memories of Bert and our relationship to disappear.

The children and I spent Thanksgiving at my sister Lisa's house with other members of the family. It wasn't easy by any means. As suggested in the support group, I took a framed picture of Bert with me and placed it on the table for everyone to see. It gave us permission to talk about him and to remember how expansive his position had been within our family circle. It decreased the awkwardness of having to avoid the subject of his absence. Of course, Thanksgiving brought to mind all the many things I had to be thankful for, and I tried to concentrate on those. The fact that Bert was in my life at all and how he had changed it for the better for my two children and me was worth remembering with gratitude and joy. He had been one of God's blessings to us.

A few days after Thanksgiving, I attended my first Rosary and funeral since Bert's. A dear friend had lost her precious year-old daughter. Even though the services brought back the deep sadness of my own tragedy, it wasn't about me that day. It was about the short life of a sweet little baby and everything the family was going through in saying goodbye to her. My thoughts and prayers were solely for them. I was reminded that without experiencing my own deep sorrow, I wouldn't have the depth of understanding required for that moment. We're quick to say, "I'm so sorry. You have my deepest sympathy," but they're empty words if we haven't suffered a loss ourselves. The next several months wouldn't be easy for them. Their faith would be tested every day, just like mine continued to be. I would try to share with them what I was learning . . . but not until they were ready to hear it. Grief and sorrow are part of our humanity and for many of us they become a legitimate companion, even while we learn to celebrate love and life in a new way.

As I sat through the Rosary and funeral services, I felt the pangs of loneliness, even while among friends. I missed the closeness Bert and I had shared during times such as this one and the warmth of his hand as he held mine. Feeling alone in a crowd wasn't a new feeling. I had often wondered if I would spend the rest of my life feeling like a fifth wheel whenever I was with family and friends, all of whom were married. It was hard to ignore that I created an "odd" number for seating arrangements at a table, for instance. Even with family, I felt separate from the others and "different."

In the early weeks of December, signs of the Christmas season were everywhere. There was no way to avoid becoming part of the hustle and bustle. Streets and stores were more crowded, holiday music blared from store intercom systems, and everyone I encountered in fulfilling my daily tasks spoke of decorating, shopping, and making plans for family gatherings. If it had been up to me, I would have ripped the month from the wall calendar altogether. So many of the traditions we had enjoyed as a family seemed like trivialities when weighed against the heaviness of my heart.

One evening, I went to a fundraiser with my sister and while I was away from home, Chris and Emily went shopping for a fresh pine tree and had it completely decorated with our collection of ornaments and lights before I returned. They even put up the Christmas lights on the outside of our house. They wanted to surprise me and remove some of the stress they had recognized through my sullen behavior. I hugged them both. "You're angels, that's what you are! My special angels! Thank you so much for doing this. Christmas *is* a special time of year and Bert would have wanted us to celebrate in the way we always do." Wiping away fresh tears, my heart swelled with pride. "I especially appreciate how you're helping each other cope with the stress this season brings. Bert's no longer part of our family circle, but his spirit will be with us because of your outward show of love. I'm so lucky to have you in my life."

The kids and I dressed in our holiday finery and went through the motions of our usual Christmas Eve customs. We prepared our assigned contribution to the family dinner, attended a special Christmas mass, and then joined family members at my sister's house. I smiled and chatted and tried to have a good time, thankful for the support and understanding of everyone present, but I remained mentally detached from the frivolity. A part of me wanted to isolate myself physically from everyone. Nothing was the same. I watched Chris and Emily and knew they were feeling awkward and sad as well. My heart ached for them. It wasn't right for them to have to deal with such tragedy at their young age. Their hugs spoke volumes, without their ever having to speak what was on their minds. They loved me and understood the difficulty involved in celebrating such a wondrous event as the birth of our Savior and how we use this gift from God as the reason to gift each other with remembrances.

On Christmas Day morning, I awoke early to begin my morning devotions. Then I turned on the Christmas tree lights, lit the logs in the fireplace, and put gifts for the kids under the tree. If Bert had been with us, there would have been many more presents to join mine, as I didn't like shopping. He thoroughly enjoyed buying special things for all of us. I prayed often throughout the day, as we made our rounds to visit with my family members and with Bert's. Again as a suggestion from the support group, we changed a few things to establish new traditions. In the past, we usually gathered at the home of my sister Lisa; this year, we gathered at my sister Laura's house. Although we had always visited with Bert's parents in the afternoon, we went in the evening instead. These few small changes made a difference, and the three of us found we could talk about Bert and reminisce about past episodes that brought smiles to our faces and laughs to soften the sadness.

The day after Christmas, the kids and I quickly took down our tree and all the decorations, packed them up and put them away for another year. We had made it through the holiday, but now were ready to put away the constant reminder of our first Christmas without Bert. We didn't need colored or twinkling white lights to remind us of the real reason for

Christmas, but while our hearts were filled with thankfulness to God for his blessings, we were human enough to fall victim to our sorrow. Fortunately, God understands more than anyone that even a strong faith goes through moments of strife. He waits for our return.

On December 27th, we joined other family members and a few friends in the celebration of my parents' sixty-second wedding anniversary, a milestone worthy of recognition. We reserved the party room at their assisted living facility and saw to it that they were attired in their best outfits for picture-taking purposes. Dad wore his customary pressed jeans and cowboy boots and hat. We brought an abundance of food choices and drinks for everyone and fresh flowers and a special anniversary cake. Lisa did most of the planning, as she enjoyed the preparations. We had in mind, as we did each year at this time, that perhaps this would be the last of such a celebration because of my parents' increasingly serious medical conditions. God had blessed us with many more birthday and anniversary commemorations than we had ever expected, but we wanted to take advantage of photographing the family each time . . . just in case. No one had ever thought at these events that the first one to leave our family circle would be Bert.

Lisa had created several photo collages over the years depicting every member of the family at various stages of their lives. Now, she had them displayed in the party room and we shared memories of the times the events had taken place. I felt incredibly blessed to have such a close-knit family; we had all received unconditional love and a never-ending supply of encouragement, support, and inspiration from our parents. I was proud of them. In their sixty-two years as the head of our family unit, they had produced six children, many grandchildren, and even great grandchildren, all of whom were present to honor them. They were truly an example of what God had intended for marriage and family relationships. They had stood by each other through years of trials, tribulations, and seemingly insurmountable obstacles.

As I studied the pictures in the collages and others scattered on the tabletop, I suddenly came across one from a previous anniversary. I was seated next to Bert and he had his arm around me. For only a few moments, I felt my heart tumble as I mourned the end of my dream of a long marriage with him. Life, in that respect, didn't seem fair.

As I drove home with the kids after the party, I knew I had one more mountain to climb before the year ended. New Year's Eve. We had usually spent the entire last week of school vacation with Bert at the ranch, where we'd observe the year's end and the beginning of a new one with a big party, complete with a roaring bonfire, fireworks, good food, and the company of family and friends.

In the darkness of the car, Emily touched my arm. "Mom, you haven't said anything about it yet, but are we going to the ranch tomorrow? I really want to, but I won't go without you. You've been great all through Christmas and tonight. I just thought that maybe —"

"I'm okay with that, Emily. I think we should go. You and Chris haven't been there since last spring. There's no sense in putting it off. If we wait until next year, we'll just be back to the beginning of missing Bert's company. I'll go for at least a couple of days. I've already mentioned it to my friends and they've agreed to go with me. Maybe having a couple of my friends along will make it seem like a different occasion. They've never been to the ranch. Showing them around will keep my mind occupied."

Chris drove himself to the ranch. The four of us women left San Antonio the day before New Year's Eve. Women are rarely without words and we found plenty to talk about on the long trip south. I was glad I had already put the first visit behind me. I knew what to expect and I hoped I could relax and enjoy this family haven, once the initial shock of my return visit was over.

Emily was quiet during most of the trip and again after we arrived at the ranch. She seemed to be all right, but I noticed she preferred to be around other family members and friends who were already on the expansive property. I rarely saw her except for the few minutes before we climbed into bed in the evenings. In addition to our house, my parents' home was on the same property. We called it the "main house," because everyone gathered there. My sister Laura and my brother Pete also had houses nearby, all within walking distance of each other, like neighbors.

Surprisingly, the days passed quickly and enjoyably. Chris and Emily really wanted me to immerse myself into the new schedule and urged me to nap in the afternoon and then greet the new year with them and everyone else. In years past, there were many times when Bert and I didn't make it to the New Year's countdown. We preferred to be by ourselves, watch a movie like any other night of the year, and mark the end of the year together.

"Come on, Mom," Emily said. "You can do it. Don't make the rest of us feel guilty for wanting to let go of 2009 and make a fresh start. You've got your friends here for a reason. Join them in greeting the new year."

"Yeah," Chris added. "Pretend you're throwing all this years' pain and sadness into the bonfire and make a resolution to look to the future rather than on the past."

It wasn't until after I had returned from our trip that the loneliness set in again. My children were right. I needed to look more toward the future. I had spent seven months living in the past and wishing I could return to it. If only I could see clearly into the future, it would be so much easier. *"Why is light given to a man whose way is hid, whom God has hedged in . . ."* Job had lamented. Gerhard Frost had written about this passage, "He [God] gives us a candle rather than a floodlight — and he promises to be there. He asks us to remember that mystery is one form of his mercy. His aim in not to keep things *from* us, but to keep things — the best things — *for* us."

The mystery of my future. Why couldn't I drum up enthusiasm, curiosity? What if I consistency stumbled? Could I pick myself up? I wanted God to flood my pathway with such radiant light I couldn't possibly make a misstep. If only I could perceive myself as I'd be six months into 2010 and know my destination. If only someone would say "do this" and I didn't have to make the decision myself. Then I'd be able to overcome my grief and greet each new day with anticipation. I was back to voicing the *if onlys*.

Regrettably, I couldn't figure out where I fit in the world anymore. I wasn't really living, only existing. I was tired of having to work so hard at everything. Would I ever be genuinely happy again? And why was it always *I, I , I*? Why couldn't I focus on the kids' futures, my parents' comfort in their last weeks or months on earth, or on figuring out how I could help others who were in far worse straits than I?

As I look back now at that bleak time in my life, I realize I had experienced many firsts as an unexpected widow and suicide survivor in those last seven months of 2009. I had coped with the pressures that came with several annual family events and holiday celebrations: Bert's birthday, my birthday, Father's Day, Mother's Day, Independence Day, Labor Day, Thanksgiving, Christmas, and New Year's Eve. While there had been plenty of tears, there had also been sweet memories of those times we'd shared as a complete family. Although I still had many more firsts in my future, I felt my past successes and God's comforting arms had armed me with some of the strength and courage required to not only endure, but thrive.

I spent New Year's Day thinking more about the future, not only for myself but for Chris and Emily, my parents and extended family, and also for Bert's parents and family. Our bonds had grown stronger through this unspeakable family crisis. I would continue to take baby steps, one day at a time, and fortify my faith and trust in God. I couldn't help but remember the words of one of Garth Brooks' most beloved recordings: *Some of God's greatest gifts are unanswered prayers.* Thankfully, God had ignored my pleas to take my life in order to avoid my pain. Many more of my prayers remained unanswered, because I wasn't ready for the next steps.

I reread a favorite passage from Ecclesiastes and prayed for patience.

> *There is a time for everything, and a season for every activity under heaven:*
> *a time to be born and a time to die, a time to plant and a time to uproot,*
> *a time to kill and a time to heal, a time to tear down and a time to build,*
> *a time to weep and a time to laugh, a time to mourn and a time to dance,*

a time to scatter stones and a time to gather them, a time to embrace and a time to refrain, a time to search and a time to give up, a time to keep and a time to throw away, a time to tear and a time to mend, a time to be silent and a time to speak, a time to love and a time to hate, a time for war and a time for peace.

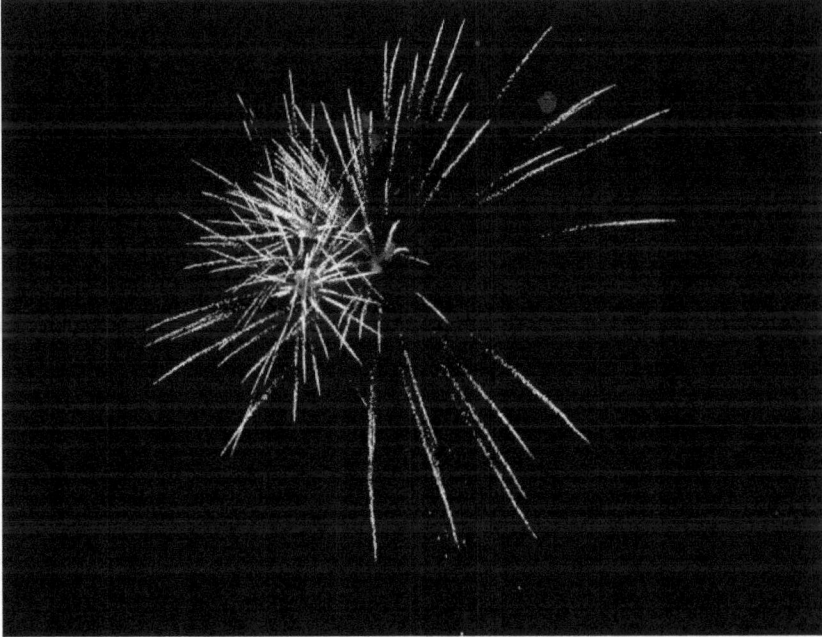

He has made everything beautiful in its time. He has also set eternity in the hearts of men; yet they cannot fathom what God has done from beginning to end. . . . I know that there is nothing better for men than to be happy and do good while they live. That everyone may eat and drink, and find satisfaction in all his toil — this is the gift of God. I know that everything God does will endure forever; nothing can be added to it and nothing taken from it. God does it so that men will revere him. — Ecclesiastes 3:1-22 (NIV)

Chapter 10

Dreams, Decisions, and Death

When you have been happily married to someone and then are suddenly alone day after day with your thoughts, writing is cathartic. It's a private way to speak with your spouse and feel the warmth of his presence, without censorship from others. This is especially important in the long evenings when busy daytime activities have dwindled and the house seems bigger and emptier. At this time of day, the silence echoes in the house and you can literally hear the ache in your heart. That's when I would write.

One day, my sister Lisa and I were talking about this. "Letty, I need to tell you something important," she said, hesitantly and as though she dreaded having to bring up the subject. "I've been putting it off, but . . ."

"What is it?" I asked, reaching out to her. "You know you can tell me anything."

She nodded and looked away. "A week or so ago, Regan was at your house waiting for Emily to get out of the shower. She was sitting on your bed and saw one of your journals lying open. She was only intending to move it further away from her, but something you had written caught her attention. She started to read the entry and found she couldn't stop. Regan feels terrible for reading something so personal without your permission, Letty, but she was so moved by it, she started to cry." Lisa hesitated again. "It was a letter you had written from Bert to you. That's why she found it so heartrending. Do you remember the one I'm talking about?"

I shook my head. "No, I can't say that I do. I've been writing every day for years and didn't stop after Bert's death. I don't remember writing anything like that, although not remembering things I've written isn't unusual, especially these days. If I ever do go back to read things from past months or years, I'm often surprised by what I find."

"Maybe you should find this letter, Letty. Regan said it really touched her heart. Young girls aren't often interested in things like that."

Later that evening, I searched through my journal for the entry Lisa described. It did surprise me. I truly had no recollection of ever writing it.

Bert, honey, is there anything you want to tell me? If so, take my hand in yours and write it with my pen.

Letty . . . First thing, know that I love you and, yes, it's me talking to you. I want you to know I am at peace. Try harder to be happy again. Please understand that my time on earth was finished. I lived my life the way it was meant for me to live it, even though the years were few. Although I didn't want to leave you and the kids, it wasn't until I reached heaven that I realized how tired I was. I lived my 41 years of earthly life to the fullest, and now I am resting in the wonder of my heavenly home.

One day in the near future, I will appear to you in your dreams, but the time isn't right yet. Please don't cry. I'm happier than I have ever been, but in a different way than you and I were happy. I didn't suffer at the time of my death, Letty. I knew it was coming, but I had already surrendered my life to God. I was ready and I knew that all would be okay with you and the kids. I was at peace when I left the world.

Continue with your life and look forward to the many wonderful things you have yet to experience. So many blessings are coming your way. Expect and be excited about them.

Don't worry about anything. Don't live with regrets or imagine things that weren't true. We both believed in the depth of our love for each other. That will never change. But just as I have moved on to my new life, I want you to do the same. God has promised we will be reunited one day and we will pick up where we left off. It will be an exciting reunion for both of us and then we'll be together for all eternity.

I still don't understand everything about my new life, but there are angels in abundance who are looking out for you, and we are all asking God to bless you and the kids. There is no such thing as time up here, so waiting for you will be quick. Try to discipline the kids the way I would if I were still with you. Don't worry about their safety. Their angels are watching out for them. And please, honey, don't be troubled about your finances. You will not run out of money. Don't worry about how long it will last. God will always provide for your daily needs. Just continue to do what you are led to do.

Live your life to the fullest and, again, please don't cry anymore. You know how I always hated to see you sad. Be patient. Everything will work out for the good of everyone. I know you miss my body, but having my spirit with you is so much better. You may not be able to understand this now, as I had no idea myself until I came into this new life. There are absolutely no words to describe how it is and how wonderful it feels to be praising God with the angels.

I am with you in spirit wherever you go. My earthly life had to end so that God's perfect and divine plan for your life could be carried out. Trust in God and have faith that He knows best. He will give you the courage and the strength you need to make it through anything. You are a strong woman, stronger than you think. Be there for the kids and your family and friends who need you. We had a beautiful and wonderful life together. One filled with so much love. We were truly blessed and as long as you believe that dying is not the end, my absence will become easier to accept. There *is* life after death, and I can't wait to experience it with you. But it's not your time yet, Letty.

As I read the letter, I sobbed quietly, believing the message had, indeed, come from Bert through one of God's miracles. The handwriting was mine, but I still have no idea where the words came from.

Later, I shared the letter with Lisa. "Letty," she said, "do something with your writing. You've been given a gift. It brings you comfort and it might bring comfort to others."

"Maybe you're right, Lisa, but it's too soon to think about that. Ironically, many years ago while I was meditating, the thought of writing an inspirational book came to me out of the blue. I knew it was God speaking to me, but I didn't know what the subject should be. I'll continue to write, pray about God's will, and see where it takes me."

A few days later, I decided that if I were destined to become a real writer — one who shared her viewpoints with others — I should have a specific place in the house designated for more purposeful writing activities. I had always chosen the corner of my bedroom on a chaise lounge, for my devotional reading, meditation, and journaling For the next few days, I busied myself by transforming the bedroom used by my parents when they lived with me into an office. First, I removed everything from the room, including the doors of the closet to make that space a "built-in" bookcase area. I applied a fresh coat of paint and installed stained plantation shutters in the windows. Then I moved in whatever dark-stained furniture I had in other rooms, such as the bookcases that I installed in the closet to hold my books, journals, and writing materials, a desk, an office chair, end tables, a beige loveseat with a variety of colorful pillows, and a brown leather chair. Once the basics were in place, I finished off the new décor with several wall crosses and inspirational plaques, some lamps, pictures of Bert and the kids, candles, incense, a table-top water fountain, an antique church kneeler, a CD player, and a vase of fresh flowers. Then I hung a special plaque on the door: "Prayer: when life gets too hard to stand, kneel." Whenever I open the door, I can immediately feel the invitation of the Holy Spirit as I am drawn into the room with a sense of peace and comfort.

With my improving outlook on life and a potential goal in mind, I finally started to accept invitations for luncheons and shopping trips with my sisters and friends; they had not stopped asking me week after week, and I knew that if I continuously declined, they would soon quit inviting me. Even though I still had occasional emotional outbursts, they were diminishing in number and intensity.

One night I met for a drink with an old friend who was also single. Although we had a pleasant conversation and a few laughs, I felt guilty. Bert had been the topic of much of our conversation, but in my heart I still felt as if I were being unfaithful to him. A part of me wanted to take such occasions in stride, but another part of me wanted to remain tied to the past. I wanted to be known forever as Bert's widow. I examined the wedding ring on my left hand. Could I wear it the rest of my life, or did I have to remove it, and if so, when? And what should I do with the ring if I removed it? Keep it in my jewelry box with other pieces? Put it in a safe deposit box to be found after my own death? Have it made into something else, like a charm to wear on a necklace?

I continued to put off a decision. Was there such a thing as wedding ring etiquette? The very thought of such a thing seemed ludicrous. My ring symbolized the emotional and everlasting commitment I had made to Bert. This commitment didn't end simply because he had died. I shouldn't have to feel pressure from others to remove it. I decided I'd continue to wear it as long as it held meaning for me.

Of course there were those who occasionally brought it to my attention. "Are you always going to wear your wedding ring, Letty?"

The question would offend me. "I might. It represents a very special time in my life."

"Won't wearing it keep other men from knowing you're available?"

"If I should ever meet someone special enough to take Bert's place, he'll understand its importance to me. He'll know I'm a widow. Such a time may never come. If I ever feel it's too difficult for me to be reminded of Bert, or if I chose to use it some other way, I'll make a decision then.

Right now, I'm not ready for that step. I don't have closure on my acceptance of Bert's death yet. God will let me know what to do and when. I'll leave the matter in His hands."

On the morning of the eighth-month anniversary of Bert's death, he was on my mind during my usual routine of praying, meditating, and writing. I talked to him. "I know you're happy, Bert. Heaven is a place where everyone is joyful and without a single burden. I wish you could give me a sign that you're with me today. On the sixth of every month, I relive that phone call that forever changed my life. I need to see your smiling face. I need something to warm my soul today."

In the kitchen a few minutes later, I was busily preparing breakfast for Chris and Emily. They both enjoy breakfast tacos and I soon had the scrambled eggs and crisp bacon strips ready. As I had for many years, I made tortillas from fresh ungrillled dough. It would never do to serve an already prepared tortilla from a store package. I soon had the first tortilla on the hot griddle. I flipped it over and gasped aloud. The tortilla had browned in the pattern of a smiley face! There it was, the clear image of two brown eyes, a nose and a broad smile. My heart skipped a beat and my next breath was literally snatched away as I stood gazing at it in awe. There was no doubt in my mind. Bert was sending me a message. He was happy and he was thinking of me.

"Chris! Emily! Come quick! It's Bert!" I turned as they entered the kitchen on a run, thinking I had finally lost my mind. "I asked him to give me a sign that he was happy and thinking of us today. Look!" I gestured at the tortilla, still on the griddle.

Christopher and Emily were speechless as they stared at the apparition. Then Chris just smiled and shook his head. Emily peered at me with wide eyes. "We can't eat that, Mom. And we can't throw it away. What are we going to do?"

To this day, that special smiley-face tortilla resides in our freezer, protected by a Baggie.

One day, during a lunch date with my friend Ana, we were discussing an upcoming ACTS retreat. I had committed myself to being on a team with her months ago because they were so inspirational. ACTS, the acronym for Adoration, Community, Theology and Service, is the precept of the retreats. They are a Catholic tradition but are open to all faiths. Usually, they are directed for and by those within a specific parish. No two ACTS are exactly alike, but they are patterned after the acts of the apostles as written about in the Book of Acts in the New Testament (Acts 2: 42-47). Participants eat, worship, share, and receive instructions together and then return to their parishes to provide loving services to others.

I had agreed to be a member of the team for the retreat, as my friend Caroline was serving as the director and Ana was her co-director. Part of their responsibility involved selecting a team of approximately twenty-four ladies to make detailed plans for the retreat months in advance. During my grieving process, I had attended several of these meetings. Now Ana had a special request.

"Letty, this is coming out of the blue, but I'm going to ask you anyway. Would you be at all interested in sharing your story at the retreat?"

I dropped my fork and stared at her with my mind racing a mile a minute. "Oh, Ana, I —I'm not sure I'm ready to do something like that. I might stand there with shaking knees and not be able to say a single word. I might collapse in another crying fit. I'd embarrass you and —"

"I just thought it might help you, Letty. I know your story would touch the hearts of so many people. The topic of the retreat is forgiveness, and both Caroline and I believe your experience these past several months would define the need to come to terms with forgiving those who have betrayed or hurt us in some way or had a profoundly negative effect on our lives."

It was as though God were speaking directly to me. Perhaps this was the beginning of my new life . . . the next major step in my journey toward purposefulness. The preparation for such a presentation had a direct bearing on why I had set up a study for myself. What good was having such a room, if I only wrote for my own benefit?

"You know what, Ana," I said. "Maybe you're God's messenger. Maybe He spoke to you to ensure I would hear Him. I've been waiting for an answer to my prayers concerning what I should do with the rest of my life. I have felt totally useless. I'm not by any means through my grieving process yet, and I'm not at all sure I'm the right one to speak as an example for anyone else, but I can be honest about my struggles. I'll ask for God's guidance through the process."

Ana patted my hand. "I know you can do it. You're ready. You have a powerful message to share."

My thoughts about what to say at the retreat had to be put on the back burner. My dad's health was rapidly declining. He didn't want to eat, he slept around the clock, and many times a day he said he was tired of living. He was ready to die. Then he'd do an abrupt turnabout. He'd proclaim he didn't want to die, or he was afraid of dying.

One Sunday afternoon, my sister Lisa and I were preparing for a trip to San Marcos for a cheerleading competition. Both Emily and Regan were participants and we wanted to enjoy the experience with them. At that very moment, Lisa received a call from the assisted living facility. "I'm sorry to report that your father fell a few minutes ago," one of the caretakers said. "We've called 911 and an ambulance is on its way here. I think you should come."

"I'm with my sister Letty. We'll be there shortly. Thank you for calling us."

When we arrived at the facility, we learned Dad had wheeled himself outdoors, probably to get some fresh air and watch the world pass by on the street. It was very windy that day, and a gust had apparently overturned his wheelchair. The staff had found him lying on the ground towards the back of the building. No one knew how long he had been there or exactly who had made the report. He was on his way to the hospital for an examination. We drove there and once we learned the doctors were going to run several tests and take x-rays, we called our other siblings. When they arrived, they urged us to continue on to the cheerleading competition. They would call us as soon as they learned something definitive. Our hearts were heavy, but we needed to lend our support to our daughters. This was an important day for them. Our dad would understand.

Dad never recovered from this trauma. Although he hadn't broken any bones, he had broken whatever spirit he had left. He simply gave up. He didn't have the energy required to bounce back. He remained in the hospital for the next two weeks, and my siblings and I took turns staying with him and watching over our mother, who didn't want to leave his side. Finally, the hospital staff said there was nothing more they could do and we'd have to move Dad to either a nursing home or a hospice facility, where they were better prepared to help the patient and family members prepare for an imminent death.

For the next week, Dad occupied a hospice bed. It was difficult to see him in his weakened and unresponsive condition. He looked fragile and small. He received morphine for the pain that came with his fall to the ground and he slept most of the time. Even when he was asleep, his eyes were wide open. The irises appeared glassy and dead, like those in a china doll. When I tried to close his eyelids over them, the lids wouldn't remain closed. "All we can do at this point is try to make your father comfortable," the hospice staff said.

I took my portable CD player to his room one day and played soft music for him, using the earphones. He seemed to be comforted by it. At the end of the week, we decided to take Dad home and have a hospice nurse remain with him there.

Over the years, we six siblings had not always agreed on matters concerning our parents. We each had our own strong and differing opinions, convinced ours were in their best interest. The added stress that comes with the impending death of a beloved parent caused a new kind of tension and the six of us could not agree on the next step. Often three of us would agree and the other three would disagree. It caused restless nights and frustrating days for me, each accompanied by renewed anxiety. Death is not a subject any of us likes to face. Our reasons are personal. We have different personalities. We deal with stress in different ways. Some people explode in easily agitated anger. Others walk about with pinched lips and keep their thoughts to themselves. Others worry, and others cry and wring their hands. Some people develop ulcers, others high blood pressure, still others heart problems.

I had been dealing with the death of my husband and thoughts of my own death for months. I tried very hard to turn my concerns over to God, once again coming to Him with pleas for immediate mercy, the ability to understand and forgive any infractions, and for answers on how to handle this new distressing crisis in our family — a crisis that involved all of us, but especially our mother.

Dad was dying. He would soon join Bert in heaven. How different the news of his death would be compared to that of Bert's. Bert was young and his death was sudden and unexpected. My father was eighty-four years old. He had lived a long and remarkable life. He was tired of living, just as Bert had been. But dying of old age is to be expected. The body parts cease to function of their own volition.

Hospice informed us of what to except in Dad's last days. "You should have your own private talks with him," our caretaker suggested. "A person's hearing is usually the last thing to go. Although he is no longer responsive, he will be able to hear everything."

Each of us had our private moments with Dad. We made amends for wrongs we thought we had committed against him and asked for forgiveness. We told him how much we loved and respected him. Still Dad held on to life. I believed he was waiting for my older sister to arrive from Dallas and have her special moment with him. Even afterward, Dad held on to life.

The hospice nurse called us together outside his room. "I know you mean well. Saying goodbye is a difficult thing to do. But sometimes when you cry and repeatedly tell him that you don't want him to die, he feels impelled to hold back. Maybe you should give him time by himself now."

I immediately became defensive. I hadn't had the opportunity to halt Bert's death. I'd had no time with him to discuss anything or to confirm the depth of our love. I didn't want to urge my father to let go and leave me. I thought the caretaker was being rude. She didn't understand. I put all thoughts of how she spent all day, every day with dying patients and their families. Our family was no different. She knew what she was talking about. Once again, I was at war with my rational and irrational thoughts before I realized what I was doing — what my siblings were doing. We needed to let Dad know it was okay for him to let go and leave us. He needed to know we would take good care of his wife, our mother. He had fulfilled his duty to all of us.

I reentered the room and leaned over to whisper in my dad's ear. "When you see Bert, tell him I love and miss him. It's okay, Daddy, take God's hand and find the rest and happiness you deserve. Your pain will be gone. You'll never suffer again. No more surgeries. No more medications. You'll have a new body. Let go now. Let your spirit fly away."

The last thing I did for my father was to leave a bouquet of fresh flowers on his nightstand. In the afternoon of February 8th, 2010, Dad passed away. I was by his side. I never thought I would have the courage to witness his death, but I am so grateful to God for remaining with me and for planning this spiritual experience. He wanted me to be present. It was part of my healing journey. Dad showed signs that he had caught a glimpse of the other side. It brought me comfort to know that Bert was there waiting for him. They had enjoyed an extraordinary relationship.

While I was seated beside Dad, I suddenly saw him open his eyes. I alerted everyone else in the room. "His eyes are open!"

"Often, right before a person dies, the eyes will open," the hospice nurse informed us.

As my mother and my siblings and I surrounded him for that second, we watched him reclose his eyes in peace and breathe his last breath.

In another six days, it would be Valentine's Day. While I was helping to prepare for my dad's funeral, I couldn't help thinking about Bert, who had been my valentine for so many years. Men were already buying flowers, cards, and bottles of wine for their significant others in the grocery stores I visited. I watched couples holding hands and realized how such a seemingly small and insignificant thing could mean so very much in a relationship. The reality of how alone I really was saddened me . . . and then I thought of my mother.

Mom had just lost her husband of sixty-two years, and because of a stroke, she had not been able to speak with him during their last twenty years. How difficult this must have been for her and for Dad. And now, after losing the love of her life, she was unable to express herself with words, only silent tears. All she could do was sit by his side and stroke his hand.

118

Not even the planning of a loved one's funeral is enough to end the bickering that comes with sibling relationships. We were a close-knit family, but we weren't exempt from wanting our way, even for such a solemn occasion. Each of us had ideas for how to best honor our father. Some wanted to have an extravagant service above and beyond the usual, while others were concerned about how to best contain expenses. Somehow, we worked it out to our mutual satisfaction, and in the end, Dad's services were beautiful and touching and a splendid way to celebrate the life and death of such an extraordinary man. Dad would have been proud.

For the Rosary, my sister Lisa prepared a slide show and chose each song specifically for him. Elva, Lisa, and I gave eulogies, each different, yet meaningful to us as individual daughters who had loved him in our unique ways. We hired mariachis to play after the Rosary, and Dad would have thoroughly enjoyed them. Mariachis are an important part of Mexican culture and San Antonio is steeped in it. The mass was beautifully conducted, and the message was inspirational and touching. The burial service, where Dad received full military honors as a WWII veteran, was something none of his children or grandchildren had ever experienced. When the military officer handed Mom the carefully folded flag of the United States and spoke to her with such tenderness and respect, it brought tears to our eyes once again.

The letter I wrote and read at the Rosary remains in a folder in my file. I bring it out every once in a while to remind me of my father and the positive influence he had on my life. Although it is personal, part of it reads as follows:

> Dear Daddy . . . to have had such a wonderful man in our
> lives for as long as we had you has been a true blessing. The
> many roles you played during your long lifetime have
> exemplified how we should live our own. Through your
> wisdom, you taught us many valuable lessons, including those
> of unconditional love, forgiveness, faith and hope. They will
> remain engraved in our hearts forever. As a World War II
> veteran, you honorably served your country, yet you were a hero
> to us in so many other ways. In the eyes of your children and

grandchildren, you not only served your country during one of its times of greatest need, but you served God and your family with equal honor.

   . . . As a family, we could not keep up with the love that seemed to flow so effortlessly and abundantly from you. You were the center of our family circle by your mere presence and your love for life inspired us. There is no way to measure how grateful and proud we are to have had such a special *welo* in the lives of our children. We will forever see a part of you in them.

   . . . As I look back on the last days of your life, every minute seems to have had significance. . . . Minute by minute, God's perfect and divine plan was being carried out exactly the way it was intended. To witness the death of your earthly body and yet feel you were being resurrected at the same time is something I will never forget. God gave me the courage and the strength I needed to be with you in your last days. I went from sitting at your bedside and begging you not to leave me, to realizing that you were ready for bigger and better things and I had to let go. . . . Only a few weeks ago, you had wanted to return to my house so I wouldn't be alone with Bert gone and Christopher away at college. You said I needed you; you wanted to take care of me. At 84 years of age, you were still being my dad and wanting to watch over me.

   In your last couple of days . . . you knew you were dying. I witnessed how you went from being somewhat afraid to acceptance and even anticipation, as it appeared that you were catching glimpses of [heaven]. You talked about the light that was still a little far away. You began talking to your parents and your brother . . . You wanted to go to mass, and talked about what you wanted to wear. You wanted a little time to be alone, and you wanted flowers.

   We did everything you asked, Dad, as we knew that you were preparing yourself for the transition into your new home. Then, after spending time with your wife and all your children . . . you slipped out of our hands and into the loving arms of God's gentle embrace.

   Immediately after you passed, we witnessed a change in the weather. It poured rain for a short time and then out came the sun. Perhaps it was your tears of joy, followed by the light signifying you had arrived at your final destination. Life holds so many mysteries.

    . . . I know that you are happy and free of any bodily suffering, and while we have been left behind, God will continue to comfort us with His everlasting love.

Few of us can argue with experience or the voice of experience. When we have lived through an event or seen something with our own eyes, we have the right to voice an opinion, although sometimes we hear others talk about their experiences and we wonder if they aren't exaggerating a little. When we read of someone who adamantly declares he has seen a UFO, we are apt to raise our eyebrows in skepticism. Despite the rants of several religious cults throughout the years who claim to have had "experiences" we find beyond our comprehension or ability to accept, when we experience the suffering and ultimate death of a loved one who worshiped God and tried to live a righteous life, we know exactly where our own faith in God stands. We believe in a Heaven and in a God who welcomes us with open arms to spend eternity in His home.

During the months following Bert's suicide and the few weeks leading to my father's death, I had my faith to rely on, even when I was plagued with doubts. Just as sure as I knew my name and knew the sun would rise every morning, I knew that since my Redeemer lived, so did Bert and my father. I believe that now. They are with our God who is available at all times to guide and comfort us, to forgive us of our sins and failings, to provide us with unending courage, and to bring us inner peace and joy if we'll just let Him.

Although many people these days have decided to believe God is nothing but a fantasy, I know He lives and loves me, because I have experienced Him. Death for believers can be overcome. I rebelled against it. I ranted and raved about the timing. I wanted to take over for God and make all the decisions. But in the end, I had to rest my case. God is in charge. His ways are not my ways.

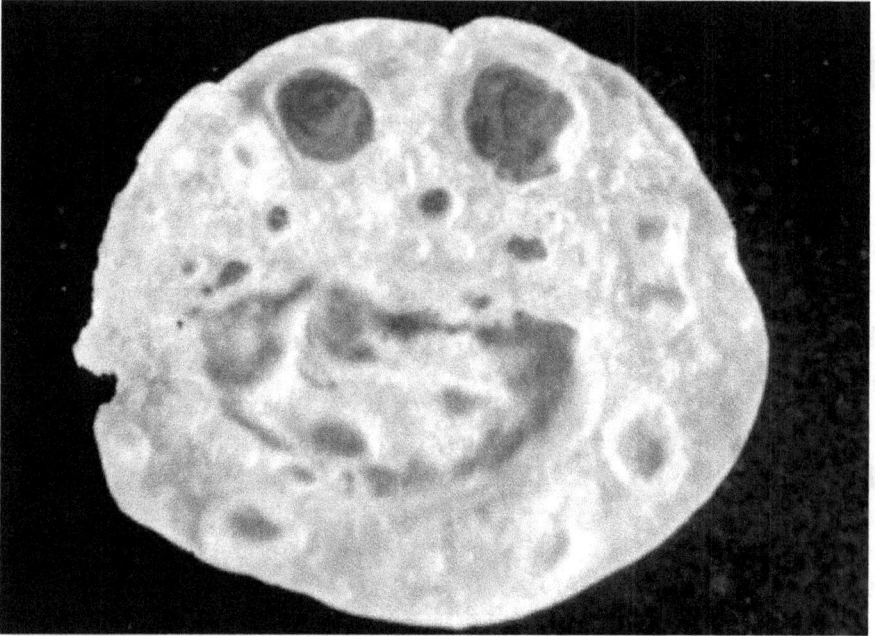

The Lord is my Shepherd, I shall not be in want. He makes me lie down in green pastures, He leads me beside quiet waters. He restores my soul. He guides me in the path of righteousness for His name's sake. Even though I walk through the valley of the shadow of death, I will fear no evil, for you are with me; your rod and your staff, they comfort me. You prepare a table before me in the presence of my enemies. You anoint my head with oil; my cup overflows. Surely goodness and love will follow me all the days of my life. And I will dwell in the house of the Lord – forever.

— Psalm 23

Chapter 11

Remembering, Persevering, Renewing

Despite the return of my former deep faith and trust in God, death seemed to hang like a pall over my house. It was almost palpable . . . a living presence that followed me from room to room. In less than a year, I had experienced the suffocating anguish that comes with the departure of a family member three times. First, I lost Bert, the love of my life; then Trout, our longtime Labrador who was a loving companion. When that elephant came crashing into my home for the third time with the death of my father, my soul was once again bared to the pain that is sharper and more enduring than labor pains; it literally sucked the life out of me. It hurts to say goodbye to those we love.

The initial tidal wave of grief that came with Bert's suicide had caught me completely by surprise. For most of my adult life, I had believed I was a wise and strong woman, perfectly capable of dealing with life's continual stresses and unexpected bumps.

I learned I wasn't.

I thought my faith in God was deep and unshakable.

I learned it wasn't.

I thought I understood and accepted the concept of a limited life on earth.

I learned I wasn't prepared for death.

Death is different. It turned my life upside down.

Death forced me to face myself in an entirely different way. It exposed a side of my character that was lacking in substance.

Death shattered my sense of being in control. It made me weak and defenseless . . . vulnerable to even the most mundane of life's daily tasks.

Death brought feelings of abandonment. Hopelessness. Uselessness. Ambivalence.

Death made me self-centered and bitter . . . and terribly lonely.

Death robbed me of my passion for living.

Death introduced me to the gut-wrenching, life-changing effects of grief.

For months, I had focused primarily on me . . . *my* heartache, *my* feelings. I had depended on whomever was on hand to "do" things for me. To pity me. To soothe and comfort me, to shower me with attention even while I wanted nothing more than to isolate myself from them in a self-imposed seclusion. I needed solitude. I wanted to remember every moment I had shared with my husband. I wanted to live only in my head and not in the world. The world was too cruel. I felt woefully inadequate to cope with its brutality.

Even while I struggled through the many phases of grief, God was with me in the darkness of my thoughts reminding me that my homes in San Antonio and Laredo, which echoed with the silence of my loved ones' voices, were only temporary havens; I was just biding my time in them until I could reach my heavenly home where I'd spend eternity.

God reminded me that the day would come when I'd never have to say goodbye again.

The impact of Bert's unexpected death, followed by the passing of Trout and my father, had a profound effect on me and, sadly, it produced repercussions that also affected my children. During these months of grieving, I wasn't one-hundred percent available for them. Physically, I was in the house. I saw them, but I didn't really connect on a deep level. We essentially passed each other like the proverbial ships in the night. I'd ask, "Are you all right?" and they'd say, "I'm okay." Of course they weren't okay. They were grieving, too, and trying to make sense of a senseless act.

Although, as I write this, I finally understand the complexity and inevitability of grief after a death, and that the benefit of such suffering for us Christians is that it brings us back to the arms of our heavenly Father for the comfort and rescue we need, I am still dismayed when I think of how I failed my children in those early months. They, too, had experienced a traumatic and significant loss and would never be the same again. They needed me. But I had lost my sense of motherly love — the kind that reaches out to protect and shield her children in their greatest time of need. The kind that has answers for their own *whys* and provides a sense of safety. The kind that reflects God's parental compassion and comfort. The kind that teaches them no one is exempt from the trials and tribulations that life brings, including the death of loved ones; but despite the seriousness of our loss, God is always present, loving, consoling, and providing the courage and strength we need to move through each day of our future. My children needed a mother who recognized how the loss of their stepfather, their much-loved companion Trout, and then their grandfather had crippled their ability to cope with the already burdensome trials that come with teenage life.

Truthfully? They had also "lost" their mother. I was too engrossed in my own heartache to do something meaningful about theirs. I had convinced myself that by taking them to a suicide support group and then to a professional therapist, I was doing the right thing. It was enough. But sending your children to strangers for comfort and answers to their questions is never enough. Not when the stunning blow of death has left them reeling. They needed their Christian mother to pray with them and to show them, through example, how they could deal with a monumental loss by going to the Comforter and developing a deeper dependence upon Him. Treading water keeps our heads above the swirling, stormy waves for only a short time until the next big wave sweeps over us. Then, like the disciples, who panicked during a storm at sea while Jesus slept, we come to realize our only savior is *the* Savior.

Thankfully, over time and with God's persistent whispers, I began to dig myself out of the pity pit and reach out to my children. I still had so much to learn, but at least I was regaining the will to try. Other things happened to reopen my eyes. After months of avoidance, I started to listen to the TV news broadcasts and read the newspapers again. Every day, I was bombarded with stories of war and earthquakes and hurricanes and tornadoes and fires. God's people everywhere in the world were going through travails, most far more devastating than my own. Suffering is universal. None of us is spared. Not in a sinful world. My personal troubles seemed more like pinpricks compared to the deep wounds of those who had lost everything they owned due to the swift revenge of a tornado or tsunami or earthquake that too often brought the loss of children or a spouse or parent. In a second, everything reminding these survivors of their life on earth was swept away. I still had my lovely home and a new and reliable car. All my belongings were intact. My children were physically healthy. We had enough money to pay bills and eat well.

I thought of the Psalmist who declared, *"You who have shown me great and severe troubles shall revive me once again, and bring me up from the depths of the earth."* (Psalm 71:20) God is gracious and good and understanding and patient. How could I have spent one minute of my time being angry and blaming Him for not preventing the deaths of *my* loved ones? What made me think I was so special? Why should I be exempt from the pain of death?

I was far from reaching the plateau of peace that comes in the person of Jesus, called the Prince of Peace by the prophets in Old Testament times, but I was definitely beginning my climb up the rocky hills to reach it, still traveling blind, but having the tight safety rope of God's promises to keep me from falling back into the chasm of hopelessness.

Now, right after the death of my father, I faced the task of sharing my still unfinished journey through grief with the women attending my church's ACTS retreat. The subject was forgiveness. My first sense was that God must be laughing at the irony. Then I found myself laughing with Him and it felt good. I had been struggling with forgiving Bert for not sharing his depression or problems with me and resorting to taking his life rather than trusting my love for him. I had been struggling with forgiving God for not preventing him from doing it and for leaving me alone to raise my children and run my household without his help. I had been struggling with forgiving God for adding to my misery with the deaths of Trout and my father. Now, after studying the Scriptures, the very thought of blaming God for my misery and then thinking I needed to *forgive Him* was a misnomer in itself; God doesn't need forgiving for anything! I wasn't in charge. I needed to seek *His* forgiveness for succumbing to the wiles of Satan instead of emulating Job and never turning my back on Him.

I returned to my Bible to read the Book of Job again. When I was through, I prayed with Job's words. *"I know that You can do everything, and that no purpose of Yours can be withheld from You. . . . I have uttered what I did not understand, things too wonderful for me, which I did not know. . . . I have heard You by the hearing of the ear, but now my eye sees You. Therefore I abhor myself and repent in dust and ashes."* (Job 42:2-6) Like Job, I asked forgiveness for thinking of God as being too small to care about someone as insignificant as me. *Now my eye sees you.* Job had expressed exactly what was happening to me. My eyes were opening and being refilled with the wonder and awesomeness of God.

The theme for the ACTS retreat was from Isaiah 43:18-19: *"Forget the former things; do not dwell on the past. See, I am doing a new thing! Now it springs up; do you not perceive it?"*

As I thought of the retreat's mission, I remembered the prayer spoken by Jesus as He taught his disciples how to pray. *Forgive us our trespasses as we forgive those who trespass against us.* If we ask for and accept God's forgiveness of our daily sins, we are expected to forgive those who have, in either great or insignificant ways, injured us. Sometimes, the injury only involves our feelings — being "put down," being taken for granted, or being made to feel unappreciated. Sometimes it involves adultery or divorce. Other times it's more serious and involves being psychologically or physically abused, often due to alcoholism or drug use in the home. And sometimes, like for me, it involves being a survivor of a suicide and needing someone to blame for the act, even ourselves.

Once I began the preparation of my presentation, I realized how grateful I was to have been asked to be a member of the team planning the

ACTS retreat. God had been in charge all along. Being omniscient, He'd known my dad would be joining Bert and other loved ones in heaven and I'd be left reeling. He'd arranged for me to be given this particular assignment at the right time in my life. I certainly had no idea how much I needed the project, even while I continued to mourn. It meant I had to shift gears. I had to go places within my heart and mind that were still hurting. I had to relive the tragedies all over again.

To remember. And remember again.

This time, however, I was ready to accept God's help and knew that He would provide all the courage and wisdom I needed for the task.

That's not to say I wasn't afraid of rustling up those feelings and emotions again. The very thought of such an exercise brought feelings of dread. It was only in believing that God had given me this task that I was able to move forward. By sharing my story with the women at the retreat, they would be helping me in my journey towards a new life. God uses people to comfort other people, especially fellow parishioners with needs similar to my own. I would persevere.

The first question I needed to define, before I could begin any meaningful presentation, was: Exactly what does forgiveness mean? The dictionary presented a list of terms that made my task seem even more formidable. *Pardon, excuse, let off, absolve, exonerate, acquit, forgive and forget.* All of those synonyms applied to what Jesus did for us when he willingly endured crucifixion to take on the resolving of our sins against God and our fellow man. Do any of us have what it takes to forgive *anyone* in the same spirit as Christ forgives us? I felt woefully inadequate and wondered how I could possibly talk about the subject at the retreat.

My thoughts were filled with questions. Was it humanly possible for surviving Jews to forgive those who ruthlessly tortured and murdered their family members during the Holocaust? Could a mother truly forgive the drunken driver who ran a stoplight and killed her only son? Could a father forgive his wife for secretly having an abortion and robbing him of the joy of raising a daughter? Could a wife forgive her husband for his deceit and lies while conducting an affair behind her back, thereby eroding the honesty and trust required of their marriage? Could a Christian employer forgive an employee for stealing money from the company after even learning the reason for the misappropriation?

Could I finally forgive Bert for taking his life rather than trusting the strength of our love to solve any problem he perceived as being too great to deal with on his own?

Since this was a Christian retreat, my major source of inspiration was the Bible. I was certainly not a theologian, but the Bible was written for people like us. In Luke 17:3-4 (NIV), Jesus was talking with his apostles about sin and forgiveness. He said, *"Watch yourselves. If your brother sins, rebuke him, and if he repents, forgive him. If he sins against you seven times in a day, and seven times comes back to you and says, 'I repent,' forgive him."*

Wait a minute. That passage made me pause. Did Jesus really mean we needed to become as altruistic as He was and humble ourselves so much we could forgive repeated hurtful actions taken against us? Wasn't that being a martyr? A willing victim? Well, wasn't that what He was?

I needed to do more research.

Gary Inrig, in his book *Forgiveness* (Discovery House, 2006) wrote something that hit home for me. I had unconsciously been using the technique for years in my sibling relationships and carried it over while wrestling with my inability to forgive Bert. Inrig said we should pay close attention to those first two words Jesus used: *watch yourselves.* "On the one hand, we need to guard against causing others to sin. On the other hand, we need to resist the temptation to keep those who have sinned against us in an emotional penalty box, making them serve endless hard time for their offenses."

Although Bert was no longer with me, I still had him in the penalty box!

During my study, I became acquainted with C. S. Lewis, a renowned 20th-century British literary and academic scholar who is considered the mostly widely read and quoted Christian spokesman of our time. Most of us know of him as the author of the well-known children's series *Chronicles of Narnia*, which have recently been made into Disney films. Lewis was formerly a self-avowed atheist, but his intellectual studies on faith led him to become a devout Christian. In his *Letters to Malcolm*, Lewis wrote two sentences on forgiveness that have stayed with me. "To forgive for the moment is not difficult. But to go on forgiving, to forgive the same offense again every time it recurs to the memory — there's the real tussle." It directly spoke to Jesus' charge that we forgive seven times seven, if necessary. It also spoke to the problem I was having. I could *say* I forgave Bert, but I couldn't *forget* his infraction against me.

I felt like a dismal failure. I had so much to learn before I could speak to the women at the retreat.

My fellow team members had arranged for a practice run of my presentation. It didn't go as well as I had planned. I was visibly and internally nervous and mumbled my speech at rapid-fire speed. And although I had practiced it several times at home, it wasn't until I was standing in front of a roomful of people that my emotions got the better of me. I wasn't at all ready to expose the intimate details of my life and dreaded the thought of disappointing my team and failing to convey the theme of the retreat. Tears hovered in my eyes, making it difficult to see the words in front of me.

My friends weren't gathered to criticize. They were understanding of my nervousness and the difficulty anyone in my position would have in expressing the pure agony that comes with the subject matter. They were there to offer support and constructive comments. One member said, "Letty, if you speak slowly and with deliberation, we can more easily soak in the feelings and thoughts behind your words as we listen. Your journey from pain to enlightenment is our journey, too. We want to hear every word. Thank you for sharing with us." Others offered equally helpful suggestions. All of them provided much-appreciated support.

After the practice run, I made a few changes to my presentation and continued to pray that God would use my story to reach at least one woman who could directly benefit from my message of hope and the need for generously giving forgiveness.

As a team, my ACTS committee members and I traveled to the Hill Country of Texas, where we stayed in a magnificent lodge surrounded by mountainous green hills, a lake, and a breathtaking vista of God's creation. Every minute of the trip there had fed my soul. To be with women who held a deep faith and abiding love for our Creator was exactly what I needed. Before the other attendees were due to arrive, we spent hours of togetherness, a few hours alone to worship and reflect, and many times of shared laughter and tears.

It was during one of our prayer services that my thoughts turned to Bert. How I longed to share this experience with him! Unexpectedly, the hole in my soul filled with an onrush of pain. My throat tightened to compress the moans that insisted upon being heard. My heart accelerated with such speed I thought it would leap from my chest. I had to get away! I had to flee as far and as fast as I could to outrun this unrelenting ache that continued to haunt me after so many months.

I excused myself and hurried outside. Then, like a long-suppressed volcano that finally spewed lava into the atmosphere, I burst into uncontrollable sobbing. What was the matter with me! I had been doing so well. I had turned my pain over to my heavenly Father. He had comforted me and reminded me of the gift of life He'd given to me. He had given me a mission to help me put things into perspective. Why had I regressed? I had failed Him. Just as I had failed my children, the other members of my family, and Bert's family, I was now failing my team members and the women attending the ACTS retreat. How could any of them possibly forgive me for being so weak? For being such a fraud?

Looking up, I caught a glimpse of two team members hurrying towards me. They gathered me into their arms, patted my back, and crooned words of comfort.

"Come back inside, Letty. We're here for you. You're just having another panic attack."

With their arms around my waist, they led me back into the lodge and placed me on a chair in the middle of the room. They and the other team members gathered around me, placed their hands over me and began praying for me. Never in my life had I experienced such a spiritual energy. As the sounds of my gut-wrenching cries continued, I heard the more quiet sobs of the other women. They were not only sharing my pain, they were letting God use the sacred moment to bring their personal pains to light. We were able to release our burdens and experience a cleansing by the Holy Spirit working through all of us. We had not scheduled this remarkable happening. God was at work, taking charge. We came to Him as one.

I will never forget that weekend with twenty-four women whose hearts were filled with a desire to be servants of God, willing to fulfill a mission we all believed He'd called us to do. Once again, I was reminded of how thankful I was to God for bringing those wonderful women into my life and for giving me the opportunity to fulfill the work he had set out for me. That's why He wants us to find a church home and to actively participate in its mission . . . to serve and reach souls in need of His comfort and assurances of a life hereafter.

I enjoyed every minute of the retreat. My responsibilities and those of my team members involved being the first ones to rise every morning and the last to go to bed, and providing every possible service for the attendees. We catered to their needs and comfort and kept the areas clean. This "doing" for others is remarkably rewarding. I learned there was little time to think about myself or my woes when my mind was focused on serving others. My presentation went very well and from the feedback I received, I know the message of hope and forgiveness inspired many. Once again, I was reminded that I can do all things through Christ who strengthens me. In serving God at the retreat, I remembered it is more blessed to give than to receive but by giving, we receive more blessings than we can count. It is through helping others that we end up helping ourselves.

One evening while on a walk in my neighborhood, not long after this weekend retreat, I listened to the quiet sounds of nature and to the silence itself and thought of Bert. I reflected on many of the happy times we had shared. It brought a feeling of quiet joy to my heart to know I could finally think of my husband without experiencing pain or regrets or anger. Letting go and letting God take over had been the best therapy for me. No statistics. No endless discussions of the phases of grief. No comparisons with how others in my position were dealing with their emotional upheaval. Just going to the Comforter and believing He would take my pain on Himself, as He always did, and replace it with memories of the joy I had experienced during my marriage was the therapy I had needed for the renewal of my soul. I had wasted so much time.

As I began the return walk to my home, I talked with Bert in my mind, telling him I was finally finding a semblance of peace, and that I had forgiven him for not sharing his pain with me and for taking his life rather than seeking medical help. I hadn't prayed for a sign from him for several weeks, but I asked him for one this time. "Anything, Bert. Some small indication to let me know you're with me in spirit, and you're happy that my spirit is being renewed and I'm finally looking forward to the rest of my life."

At that very moment, I glanced ahead of me on the street. There, sitting on the pavement and as visible as a full moon on a dark night, was a golf ball. I peered about me and felt a chill crawl up my back. Why in the world would there be a golf ball on the street — a street that was nowhere near a golf course? Bert was an avid golfer. Was this . . . ? I just smiled and hurried to pick it up.

The rest of the way home, I thanked God for being fully aware of my troubles, for never abandoning me, for reassuring me that one day I would join Bert and my father in paradise. I had been lost, but now was found. He had planned something wonderful for my future and I would share it with my children. *"You, who have shown me great and severe troubles, shall revive me again. . . . You shall increase my greatness, and comfort me on every side."* (Psalm 71:2 0-21)

I would have no more need for tears or fears.

> *And when you stand praying, if you hold anything against anyone, forgive him, so that your Father in heaven may forgive you your sins.* —Mark 11:25 (NIV)

> *Bear with each other and forgive whatever grievances you may have against one another. Forgive as the Lord forgave you.* — Colossians 3:13 (NIV)

> *How can you say to your brother, 'Brother, let me take the speck out of your eye,' when you yourself fail to see the*

plank in your own eye? You hypocrite, first take the plank out of your eye, and then you will see clearly to remove the speck from your brother's eye. — Luke 6:42 (NIV)

If we confess our sins, he is faithful and just and will forgive us our sins and purify us from all unrighteousness. If we claim we have not sinned, we make him out to be a liar and his word has no place in our lives. — John 1:9-10 (NIV)

Chapter 12

Curative Comfort

Not long after the retreat, I was sitting outside on the back porch enjoying signs of the arrival of spring. It comes early in San Antonio, often during the latter week of February. By March, many trees have already sprouted new leaves and the mountain laurel, decorative pear, and tulip trees are in full and glorious bloom. On this particular day, the stunning beauty reminded me there is a season for everything, and spring brings with it a renewal or rebirth of everything in nature. Springtime could bring a new beginning for me, too.

Just as I accepted the changing of the seasons, I could accept the changes in my life by letting go of the weeds and dead leaves of the past year and by looking forward to the donning of new clothes that represented a revitalized self-image, like wearing a new dress on Easter Sunday. If I could embrace the process and become energized by the grace of God, just like the sun energized me each morning during my early repasts, my personal renewal could prepare me for an enjoyable summer with my children . . . despite the coming anniversaries of events we dreaded having to relive.

Just then, I happened to glance at my hands and noticed the wedding ring still on my left hand where Bert had placed it during our marriage ceremony. Did it represent one of the "ornaments" of a past season? I had wondered the same thing weeks ago, but not made a decision. Was it time? I reflected on the day and manner in which it was given to me. In our vows, Bert and I had repeated the well-known phrase that we would remain married *'til death do us part.* Death had parted us. In my mind, however, we were still and would always be married. Would continuing to wear my ring keep me from moving forward? Would I be stuck in winter, unable to find joy in the upcoming spring and other seasons of my life?

Before I reentered the house, I decided to experiment with wearing the ring on different fingers. I would still have the meaningful remembrance to provide comfort when I needed something extra to get me through certain difficult days, but it would allow me to put the ring and what it represented into its proper perspective. It would be a positive step toward "letting go" and planting one more seed to bring bloom into my future.

March was a busy month. Emily had the usual high school events, including cheerleader tryouts, Drivers Ed, parties, and spring break activities all spurred by the typical hormonal changes that bring such angst to teenage girls. Chris struggled with college issues, finding one class very difficult, eventually dropping another, while trying to find himself and learn what he wanted to do with the rest of his life. Both children found their persistent grieving over our losses affected their ability to be carefree or focused. Coping with their vacillating feelings brought many "down" days.

Since the retreat, I was having better days. Clearly, turning my pain over to God and continuing with my prayer and meditation time with Him was making a difference. I learned, however, that being a devout Christian and trusting God to bring the comfort and strength and courage I needed to get through each day didn't mean my very human emotions didn't get in the way. I had to remind myself continuously that grieving takes time. Healing takes time. Understanding and earnestly forgiving takes time. Thankfully, God knows our humanness. Look at how patient he was with Job!

Lest anyone think I am a role model as a suicide survivor, I will confess that even after ten months, I had Bert's phone number in my cellphone directory, his clothes in our closets, his personal effects exactly where he'd left them, and my wedding ring on one finger or another.

There were still things I simply could not do. They seemed too final. A part of me wanted to continue living in the past. If I moved on, there would be no turning back. I wasn't ready for a spring cleaning of Bert from my physical home.

And all the while spring brought increasing lush, green foliage and grass and colorful flowers to decorate my outside world, certain dates on the calendar hovered in my mind like vultures waiting to swoop down and destroy any progress I had made.

Easter arrived on April 4th, almost one month to the day before the one-year anniversary of Bert's suicide. The anticipation of a return of the pain and suffering we'd endured for months almost clouded our remembrance of all that Easter symbolized for us as Christians. Emily and I readied ourselves to attend church services. Christopher awoke and decided he didn't want to do anything or go anywhere. He needed time to be alone. Schoolwork and college activities had created their own kind of stress and he needed to let all that go and focus on missing Bert. I knew his heart was hurting and respected his wishes. Everyone copes differently.

Easter heralds the advent of spring, of course, but there is so much more. During the church service, I was reminded that the Easter cross and lamb symbolized the crucifixion and resurrection of Jesus Christ, as did all the lit candles in the sanctuary. The colors of the altar cloths had changed from the purple of Lent to the black of Good Friday and then lily white of Easter, representing the pure life and hope we can have because of Jesus' sacrifice on our behalf and if we choose to accept His gift. The gold trim reminded me of the eternal light He brings into the world and our lives as He drives away the gloom of our dark days. I needed that hope more than at any other time of my life. So did Emily and Christopher.

After the service, Emily and I went to Bert's sister's house for an Easter buffet and enjoyed watching the youngest children hunt for hidden eggs. As always, being surrounded by loving family members who shared the same sadness was uplifting. We didn't need to talk about the tragedy that still haunted us. I considered having "family" a blessing at a time like this, although the distraction the holiday activities provides isn't always what's most needed. Later, I learned that Christopher had gone to the cemetery while we were at church. It brought me comfort to know he had followed his heart.

After leaving the get-together, Emily and I followed our own hearts and made a visit to the cemetery as well. It didn't seem right to leave Bert or my dad out of the specialness of the day. The reality of Bert's death was made even more real, because his headstone had finally been put in place. Seeing his name carved in granite brought a sweeping sense of sadness, but I remembered that because of Jesus' resurrection from His grave so many centuries before, I would be with Bert in Paradise some day. I breathed a prayer of thanks to my Savior for making this hope possible.

Easter was the most challenging for me. It was not only the first holiday without the presence of my dad, but it was also the last holiday Bert and I had shared. Someone mentioned to me once that the second year is even more difficult than the first, because each holiday triggers particular memories and the days seem rather hollow without the voices and laughter of those we loved. I had to believe that if I chose to focus on my gratitude to God for His many and continued blessings, I could participate in family, church, and community events without being overcome by the sorrow that always lurked deep in my heart. I wanted to create new traditions with my children, ones they would remember with fondness as adults with their own families.

With all the drama going on in my life and the time I'd spent preparing for and attending the ACTS retreat right after my dad's funeral, I felt I had not been a strong enough support system for my grieving mother, who had also lost the love of her life. I hadn't mourned with her and talked about Dad in ways that would bring consolation. While observing her on Easter Sunday, I both saw and felt the depth of her sorrow, which she had to endure in silence.

My sisters and I talked about it and decided we should do something that would bring her pleasure . . . something she and our father would do on occasion. We decided to drive her to Lake Charles in Louisiana, a couple of hundred miles from San Antonio, a place she had enjoyed many times over the years. It's a historic city built around Lake Charles and overlooking the beautiful Contraband Bayou. With natural habitats, fresh water marshes, scenic rivers, and inviting sunsets, we felt a long weekend there would be relaxing for all of us, and the car trip itself would provide an opportunity for Mom to have the undivided attention of her daughters. Although she couldn't participate in our chatter, because of her speech loss, she would enjoy listening to us. And, we could spend a couple of hours in one of the casinos and let her play the nickel slot machines, something she had enjoyed doing and could still manage, despite her stroke and its residual effects.

Bert and I had driven to Lake Charles on several occasions over the years. Both he and my dad would be happy to know Mom and I were making the effort to take such a trip. Still, I felt a little anxious. Being there would bring up memories of happier times. Was I ready for that? The day after Easter, April 5th, was my wedding anniversary. I had vivid memories of my marriage ceremony in Las Vegas. I had been crazy in love and so happy. Now I was a widow at the age of forty-seven. I couldn't help wondering if Bert and I would have been driving to Lake Charles together to celebrate our special day. We had thoroughly enjoyed such road trips. A long one never seemed arduous, because our talking and laughing never stopped. Being together was part of the fun. Whenever we stayed in one of the resorts, Bert would rise early to play golf and then meet me in the casino afterwards. This year, my sisters and I would make the trip with our mother.

The trip wasn't the same, but I found myself enjoying the fellowship of my sisters and the presence of our mother. I couldn't remember the last time we had spent such a protracted time together, without having spouses or children with us. We found no end of things to talk about, including laughable tales of our childhood days. Mother had an almost permanent smile on her face. Here we were. Two women whose hearts were heavy with grief over the loss of our husbands. But neither of us could fail to appreciate the splendor of spring, and every mile brought new sites to exclaim about.

After returning from Lake Charles, Chris met me at the door. "Guess what I found?" he asked, more animated than I'd seen him in a long time. "I ran across some videos of Bert. You've gotta see them, Mom. It was so great hearing Bert's voice and seeing him doing stuff. It was almost like he was still with us."

I could feel the blood drain from my face. "Oh, son, I'm not sure if I'm quite ready for that yet. Would you mind if I put that off for a while? I'm so glad they've brought you joy, though."

Although I didn't say so at the time, the very thought of watching the videos scared me. I have no idea why. All I knew was that I was not ready to take that step. To see Bert walk and talk would be worse than merely seeing or hearing him in my mind. Again, it showed me how we are each individual in how we deal with our personal grief. We can't make comparisons. We can't tell someone to move on or "get over it."

Surviving my dad's death and funeral, surviving the reliving of my sorrow in order to prepare for the retreat, enduring the sadness that came with Easter, knowing it was the last holiday Bert and I had shared, and then living through my first wedding anniversary without my partner had been emotionally draining. The whole process of grief is utterly and inexplicitly exhausting. It doesn't matter if the grieving is due to a death or any other kind of loss . . . heartache literally takes the stuffing out of you.

The many secular books about grieving mention the phases of grief made famous in Kübler-Ross's book about the subject. Although I suffered through most of the phases mentioned, I found that my grief wasn't at all straight and orderly. It was replete with twists and turns, detours and roadblocks, ditches and unpaved or rocky roads. The same feelings and emotions would return time and time again, even while I prayed that God would take them from me and leave me whole and happy once more. Again, I felt like a failure and a fraud.

I wasn't, of course. My mind and my heart knew what I was ready to accept and when. Everything would come to fruition in good time. That I wholeheartedly believed.

Everyone in my family — and in Bert's — was fully aware of what I was going through during the month of April. They knew May 6 was drawing closer and they were eager for me to be ready for it. When I received an invitation to visit Bert's sister Lisa and her family in Arizona, I jumped at the chance.

Once again, I learned that God works in mysterious ways. Although Bert and I had wanted to spend time with his sister who lived so far from San Antonio, things always got in the way for both families. Since his death, I had first become close to Lisa by spending time in phone conversations, then during our trip to Laredo to confirm whether or not Bert's death was due to suicide or murder. Spending time with her and her family was exactly what I needed. We talked, laughed, and cried. We reminisced about how things used to be and offered each other hope for our futures. We learned a great deal about ourselves and each other. We both wished we had spent time together while Bert was living, yet we knew his death is what had brought us together. Lisa's family reminded me of my home life with Bert . . . one that is radiant with love as every member participates in the giving and sharing. How blessed they were and what a blessing they were to me now. By following the Lord's guidance, we were able to fill a few of the little holes in our hearts. The healing process was working.

I had made arrangements with St. Mark's Church to hold a prayer service for Bert in its chapel on May 5, 2010. Members of our immediate family gathered for mutual support, for God's blessing, and for a time of remembrance. Even though the very reason for the service was difficult to absorb and we each experienced heartfelt sadness, we rejoiced in knowing that Bert was with the Father who had created him.

After the service, we went to a local restaurant to share breakfast and reminisce even more about Bert. Later that day, I went alone to visit his grave at the cemetery. The bench next to his headstone looked all too familiar. I had sat on it many times throughout the year reflecting on my life with this remarkable man and how much I had loved him. I thanked God once again for His grace and love, and for providing all the courage and strength I had needed to survive a full year of living, after being crushed by the blow of that one unexpected phone call. God and His truths had provided the most effective medication I'd taken for the healing of both my soul and my body as I dealt with the effects of profound sorrow.

And the filling of God's prescriptions came free for the asking. No medical insurance was needed. There was no reason to dip into my savings account or checkbook. God accomplished for me what I was unable to do on my own or through the expensive purchases of secular advice books and professional therapy.

As I talked with Bert, I confessed that the anticipation of the one-year anniversary of his suicide had been more difficult than the day itself. Why? Because of God's persistent and curative comfort, and because, in my heart, it didn't really matter what day, month, or year it was. I hadn't loved him on a timetable. I had loved him unconditionally and would love him forever.

A line from one of Alfred, Lord Tennyson's poems slipped into my mind just then, but all I could remember was the one line. I looked it up later. The entire short stanza is:

> I hold it true, whate'er befall;
> I feel it when I sorrow most;
> 'Tis better to have loved and lost
> Than never to have loved at all.

Lord Tennyson wrote the very long poem, "In Memoriam A.H.H," in 1865, upon the death of a dear friend from a cerebral hemorrhage. It is considered one of the great 19th-century poems and was a favorite of Queen Victoria. Bert was the central figure in my adult life. He will only be with me in spirit during my remaining days on earth; but I can echo Tennyson's words with firm conviction: It was far better for me to have loved and lost Bert than never to have had him in my life.

As for my future . . . I have placed it in God's hands.

For I know the plans I have for you," declares the Lord, "plans to prosper you and not to harm you, plans to give you hope and a future." — Jeremiah 29:11

Countless times over the past two years since Bert's suicide, people have asked me how I was able to recover from the shock and epic grief that comes with such a mind-numbing death. They wonder why I'm not bitter. After I summarize the travails of my arduous healing journey to assure them my road was very bumpy, I remind them that the death of any loved one under any circumstances is devastating. I mention my dad. Then their conversation extends to the death of a child by suicide.

"It's such a cruel fate," they say. "Why didn't God spare the Christian parents from their insufferable pain by sparing the life of the one whose absence has left such a gaping hole in their heart? Is faith in vain? Why do Christians have to suffer like anyone else?"

"God has gifted us with the ability to make choices," I remind them. "Our loved ones made a choice based upon their mental condition at the time. They saw no other way out of their personal agony. Now, we have the choice to let this tragedy ruin the rest of our life or to find a way to use the experience to grow in our faith and to, perhaps, help others who are finding it more difficult to forgive and move forward."

In the two years of my tussle with grief, I read through the Bible five times. Each time, I found something special I needed for just that moment — something I didn't remember reading before. Although I have quoted many verses in this book that helped me to cope on difficult days and to grow in my understanding of why a "good" God allows any sort of suffering while we're living our earthly lives, one verse stands out in answer to this particular haunting question: What meaningful lesson did I learn through Bert's death and why was it different from the death of my dad?

> *The righteous perish, and no one ponders it in his heart;*
> *devout men are taken away, and no one understands that*
> *the righteous are taken away to be spared from evil. Those*
> *who walk uprightly enter into peace; they find rest as they*
> *lie in death.* — Isaiah 57:1-2 (NIV)

I like another translation of this verse better. It comes from the New Century Version of the Bible, a more recent translation than the New International Version, which I have used throughout this book.

> *Good people are taken away, but no one understands.*
> *Those who do right are being taken away from evil and are*
> *given peace. Those who live as God wants find rest in*
> *death.* —Isaiah 57:1-2 (NCV)

That's it, in a nutshell, isn't it? As a believer, I knew that death comes to us all. I knew that none of us lives a day longer than God has planned, and that we will spend eternity with Him and with our loved ones. I will see Bert and my dad again. I was prone to forget that, especially when I was in the throes of grief, but, in time, my wounds were healed as I put my earthly life into perspective. We're here temporarily, not forever. Recently, a woman put this into a very succinct phrase for me. Our earthly life is like a comma when we consider eternity. A mere speck in a sentence.

Throughout my long journey as a suicide survivor, the support of my family and friends has been critical. During the first several months, when I felt abandoned by Bert, I needed to know those closest to me wouldn't abandon me, too. That was a very deep and constant fear. Day after day, when the house emptied as supporters returned to their own homes and families, the feeling of being alone was reinforced. Those were the darkest days. The days I was alienated from God by my own choice and needed people around me, even though I was incapable of responding to them in any meaningful way. I can say with unqualified conviction now, two years later, that I first needed God's comfort and then I needed those who were willing to sit by my side and listen with their hearts or to help with mundane chores. I am grateful to everyone who loved me during my long journey of survival.

My life has changed since that fateful day. I've changed as a mother, a sibling, a friend, and as a child of God. The changes are for the better. They have made me more honest and forthright, less pretentious and shallow. I am reminded of the many weeks when I didn't have the energy or knowhow to move from point A to point B, and when I was mentally absent from my children's lives, unable to provide the assurances and spiritual hope they needed. I have moved slowly from a state of helplessness and fear to one of more confidence and gratefulness for what each day brings.

And I'm more mindful of how I communicate my thoughts. Although the adage "Sticks and stone may break my bones, but words can never hurt me" is true in a way, we all learn through experience that words can often wound our spirits and self-esteem in a way that cripples our ability to live a fruitful life. A broken bone can be mended and even forgotten, but hurtful words can haunt us forever. I don't want to say anything that might cause another person to feel unworthy of living in this world.

I give full glory to God for never leaving my side. Without His daily guidance, I could never have reached the point of loving my life again. I still miss my husband and the children miss their stepfather. He was the center of our home and we enjoyed every year we had with him, but God is the soul of our home. Through His grace, we are able to continue our own life journeys without Bert's physical presence. He remains in our heart and we have learned to talk about him and laugh about our memories of fishing and hunting trips with him and especially about our days spent at the ranch without becoming depressed. We choose to believe that God loaned Bert to us at a special time in our lives when we needed him. I think Chris said it best. "Mom, Bert came into our lives out of nowhere. Just like an angel, he got us through tough times. He was there for us when we needed him and taught us things that helped shape our character. And then he left when his work was done. Maybe God intends to use him elsewhere."

Things happen. Things we don't expect. Tragic things. Severe illnesses, unexpected accidents, loss of income or a job, or a tornado that destroys our home in the blink of an eye. Regardless of what trials life hands us, I've learned the earth continues to turn on its axis and God is still on His throne. I view my existence differently now. Little insignificant things don't take on as much importance. I can laugh at my failures rather than becoming nonsensically frustrated. I can meet the everyday problems that once sent me spinning (like plumbing or car troubles!) with more patience. They are eventually solved. Thankfully, there is expert help available if I ask for it. And I do.

Today, I am more focused on becoming the spiritually grounded person God intends for me to be. I prayed long and hard for an answer to what God wanted me to do with the rest of my life and how He wanted me to honor and serve Him. I wanted to do something worthwhile and lasting . . . something that would speak to my children about my faith and that could become a legacy of sorts for them and for my future grandchildren. God inspired me to be more creative and to use all the gifts and talents He has given me. I began writing about the growth of my faith and how God had saved me from a lifetime of crippling grief. I started to share my thoughts on the Internet. Because I had suffered deeply, I had empathy for those who were going through the same or similar pain. I reached out to them and offered my hand in friendship to help them through their own struggles. They have sent heartwarming responses in return.

Someone asked me one day where my "ideas" came from. I believe every word comes from my heart where God places them. It is the Holy Spirit working within me who gives me inspiration to put words on paper and then the courage to send them off into the unknown with the hope of reaching just one suffering person. I believe God has chosen me for a reason I don't fully understand. I believe He has also given me the inspiration to write my story in this book for the same reason — others need to know that it's okay to blame Him when a suicide tears their life to shreds. They need to know He's patient and will remain by their side with open arms until they find their way back to Him.

Living in Texas, I've learned that if we have nothing but sunshine and blue skies and no rain, the result is likely to be in the form of a severe drought. If everything in our lives is perfect, we think we don't need God. All too soon, we yield to temptation and focus on things that don't have lasting value. We aim for showy displays, like acquiring a fancy car, a big home in the suburbs, a gold watch, a substantial savings account, and a country club membership, like so many around us. If we watch the news, however, we know how easy it is to lose them all. An earthquake, a tsunami, a tornado can take everything we have. An economic crisis can result in a long recession and the quick emptying of our savings account or the loss of our job. When we are left with nothing, we are often abandoned by those who offered their friendship based upon our show of success. These "sunshine" things spoil us. When they disappear, like the homes in foreclosure during a recession, we can become miserable and unhappy.

How much better it is, I've learned, to clothe our hearts in the security of God's promises. He looks on our hearts, not our outward appearances. That's what I want to teach my children. That even though He tests the sincerity of our faith and the genuineness of our trust by allowing the entry of thunder and lightning and hurricanes and tornadoes in the form of trials and temptations — and even the suicide of our loved one — He gets us through them feeling stronger and braver and more centered. We learn patience and persistence and to never abandon our hope for an eternal life with Him.

It took Bert's unexpected and tragic death to bring me back to the One who created me.

My heart aches for all suicide survivors who have tried for many years to come to terms with their grief. Many have withdrawn into themselves and continue to attend grief counseling and support groups, hoping they will eventually be able to move on and enjoy whatever time they have remaining in this world. All too many have not gotten over their need to blame themselves or their spouse for the suicide of their loved one. Their marriages break up. They leave their jobs and withdraw from any pleasurable new experience that might reignite their sense of guilt. Some commit suicide themselves to put an end to their suffering. My heart aches, because they don't understand that by turning to their Creator and the only real Comforter, they will receive understanding and consolation in abundance. God's support is available 24/7, free of charge.

I believe that nothing happens by accident. There is a reason for all the events that take place in our lives. I believe we are all connected to each other by the Holy Spirit and when something happens in one of our lives, it has a ripple effect that extends far beyond our reach. It causes things to happen in other people's lives and in their hearts. And it continues to be passed on from one person to another. That's why I write. That's why I reach out.

I know that God has bigger plans for me. I am excited as I wait and witness the miracles that are surely going to come my way. During my journey of agonizing grief to a stronger faith, I have enjoyed the benefits of several new challenges that have been growth experiences. I stumble and fall, but get up and keep going. I make mistakes and learn from them. I lose some things I thought were important to me, and then I'm blessed with new things I never expected. The hardest thing to conquer for me has been the fear of letting go of the past — fear that I would forget the way things used to be. I wanted to hold on to every memory and rationalized that keeping objects around me would ensure they remained fresh.

Every obstacle, every change, every significant turning point in our lives must be dealt with by the strength of our faith in God, not with our own eyes. We must have faith first, and then He will allow our eyes to see miracles we could never have imagined. My eyes have seen that neither I nor anyone else was responsible for Bert's death.

My children and I remain very close to Bert's family. We all miss the way our lives used to be, but we're embracing our past and looking forward to the changes that come with time. We think more of Bert's life than his death now. We have setbacks, of course, but they don't throw us off kilter. We have learned to talk about our feelings and to deal with issues as they happen. Both children are reading their Bibles and seeking God's guidance for their lives.

149

> *Forget the former things; do not dwell on the past. See, I*
> *am doing a new thing! Now it springs up; do you not*
> *perceive it?* — Isaiah 43:18,19a (NIV)

In order to take a forward step into my brave new world, I took a job at a local flower shop and worked there for a year. To my amazement, I thoroughly enjoyed it and, now, I have established a personal florist home-based business I call Forget Me Not Flowers. I am taking business classes at a local junior college and also classes in floral design. I enjoy working with people and God has shown me how I can make a living by helping them through the beauty of floral arrangement in their times of joy and also the times of sadness that comes with the death of a dear one. Each flower is a miracle of creation.

My sister gave me her piano and I intend to take piano lessons. I continue to write and speak whenever I am invited to share my story of hope. I am enjoying a rich and full life again.

> *Trust in the Lord and do good; so you will live in the land,*
> *and enjoy security. Take delight in the Lord and he will*
> *give you the desires of your heart. Commit your way to the*
> *Lord; trust in him, and he will do this: He will make your*
> *righteousness shine like the dawn, the justice of your cause*
> *like the noonday sun. Be still before the Lord, and wait*
> *patiently for him.* — Psalm 37:3-7a (NIV)

It took a good two years, but I have at last started the process of going through Bert's personal things. His golf shirts went to a brother, his cowboy boots to a nephew, and many of his other things to Christopher, who finally grew into them and enjoys the memories that come with each wearing. I have saved several shirts and intend to have someone create memory quilts for Bert's mother, Emily and me. Bert's pictures will remain in place, next to those of my dad.

God is my constant Companion. I am never alone. Ever. And as the weeks and months and years of my journey toward a new life progress, I know He will continue to encourage me each step of the way. He will do the same for you! God will carry not only us, but all our burdens.

Even to your old age and gray hairs I am he, I am he who will sustain you. I have made you and I will carry you; I will sustain you and I will rescue you. — Isaiah 46:4 (NIV)

. . . God has said, "Never will I leave you; never will I forsake you." So we say with confidence, "The Lord is my helper; I will not be afraid. What can mere mortals do to me?" — Hebrews 13:5-6 (NIV)

And we know that in all things God works for the good of those who love him, who have been called according to his purpose. — Romans 8:28 (NIV)

Leaning on the Everlasting Arms

What a fellowship, what a joy divine,
Leaning on the everlasting arms;
What a blessedness, what a peace is mine,
Leaning on the everlasting arms.

Refrain:
Leaning, leaning, safe and secure from all alarms;
Leaning, leaning, leaning on the everlasting arms.

Oh, how sweet to walk in this pilgrim way,
Leaning on the everlasting arms;
Oh, how bright the path grows from day to day,
Leaning on the everlasting arms.

What have I to dread, what have I to fear,
Leaning on the everlasting arms?
I have blessed peace with my Lord so near,
Leaning on the everlasting arms.

Refrain

This well-known hymn began as a poem written by Elisha A. Hoffman back in 1887. After learning that the wives of two friends had died, Anthony J. Showalter wrote the score and words to the refrain, and he asked Hoffman to write the remaining lyrics.

Of possible interest to many, the hymn was sung in the 1943 movie *The Human Comedy*, starring Mickey Rooney; it was nominated for Academy Awards in five categories, including Best Picture and Best Actor. William Saroyan won Best Original Story for the film.

[*The Glad Evangel for Revival, Camp, and Evangelistic Meetings* (Dalton, Georgia: A. J. Showalter & Company, 1887)].